Book of
Marine Fishes

by Hillary Hauser

🐟 Pisces Books / Tetra 🐟 Press

For Billy

Acknowledgments

It would be absurd of me to pretend that I wrote this book myself, because were it not for the help of very knowledgeable ichthyologists there would be no book at all.

In particular, Dr. John Randall of the Bishop Museum of Hawaii has provided close and steady support throughout the years that the Fish of the Month series has run in *Skin Diver Magazine,* and Dr. Randall undertook the monumental task of checking the bulk of the manuscript for this book. If there are any mistakes in this book they are entirely mine and not his, since much of the text had to be checked without the benefit of photographs.

Dr. Carleton Ray also provided invaluable support, advising me often over the years concerning the fishes I was writing about. Other scientists who took time to help are: Charles C.G. Chaplin, who advised on several fishes in addition to authoring one of the most definitive books on fishes (together with the late James E. Bohlke); Dr. William N. Eschmeyer of the California Academy of Sciences; Dr. C. Richard Robins of the Rosenstiel School of Marine and Atmospheric Sciences, University of Miami; Dr. Gerald R. Allen, of the Western Australian Museum; Dr. Victor G. Springer, of the Smithsonian Institution; Dr. John F. McCosker of the Steinhart Aquarium; Dr. William F. Smith-Vaniz of the Academy of Natural Sciences, Philadelphia; Richard Rosenblatt of Scripps Institution; Shane Anderson and Milt Love, both of the University of California at Santa Barbara Marine Science Institute.

Also advising me on various aspects of the book were Ben Victor and Al Ebeling of the University of California at Santa Barbara, and Dan Gotshall, a California Department of Fish and Game biologist who checked the California fish texts. Indispensible to the production of the manuscript itself were Diane Brewer and Becky Davis. There is also Art Smith to thank, for his drawings; Erv Rosen of Petersen Publishing Company, who for years worked to bring the book project to fruition; and Herb Taylor, who had the insight to proceed with the project. I also owe a great debt of gratitude to Paul Tzimoulis, publisher of *Skin Diver Magazine,* for allowing me to write the series.

Finally, I want to thank Billy Graham, who proudly introduced me to presidents and heads of state as the "writer of the Fish of the Month." To this day I can remember these dignitaries reacting to this announcement with awe and incredulity.

The photograph on the title page is of a **Blue-Blotch Butterflyfish (Chaetodon plebeius).** Often called the Two-Spot Coralfish, it is a native of Australia's Great Barrier Reef and the Coral Sea. Photo taken in 35 feet of water on Marion Reef in the Coral Sea, using a Nikon F in a Niko-Mar housing and Bauer E252 strobes in Farallon/Oceanic housings. Shot at f/16 at 1/60 second, 18 inches from the subject. Photo by Carl Roessler.

Drawings by Art Smith & Leslie W. Barrows

Library of Congress Catalog Card No.: 83-063356

ISBN: 0-86636-021-2

Printed in Hong Kong
10 9 8 7 6 5 4 3

Contents

Author's note: *The fishes in this book are presented in phyletic sequence—in evolutionary order from primitive forms to the more complex forms. This natural order follows the Linnaean system of classifying plants and animals.*

Foreword

How better to record the varied splendor of the sea than by such books as this? Although the portraits of fishes presented here illustrate but a tiny portion of the hundreds of thousands of species of marine life, they are sufficient to inspire us and to remind us of our responsibilities as stewards of this planet.

Hillary Hauser, the remarkable and energetic writer of the accounts, has here assembled a volume that reflects two very recent developments. One, of course, is the technology that has allowed these photographs to be taken. The photographs span but a little more than a decade, and underwater photography is only a few decades older. Second, a new awareness of the sea speaks forcefully of how inappropriate the name "Earth" is as a title for our water planet. As the exploration of outer space has expanded our vision of our whole planet, so the exploration of inner space has stripped away a surface shield, allowing us to see the worlds below.

I have no doubt that these two developments will, historically, be seen at the level of two previous shifts of perception—that of the Agricultural Revolution of about 4,000 years ago and that of the two-centuries-old Industrial Revolution. Through these revolutions were created civilizations, cities, automobiles—and air pollution, depleted fisheries, and ocean dumping grounds. The "Marine Revolution"—a term I coined a bit over a decade ago by analogy with the other two—will surely have no lesser impact. For, at last, humankind is becoming capable of using this entire planet. It is essential that we care for and understand the sea, as we have not the land, as we use it. Otherwise, what we see within these pages cannot flourish.

I write this introduction just following a cruise of the Chukchi Sea, on the fringes of the Arctic Ocean. My colleagues and I were rewarded by the sight of abundant gray whales, seals, and walruses. As we departed Nome, Alaska, I was reminded that Hillary's grandparents met, married, and lived there during the Gold Rush days just following the turn of the century. So, I cannot help but be struck by the realization that this book includes only fishes of warmer places where, understandably, most divers congregate. Few may be aware that the sea life of polar regions is often no less spectacular—white-blooded fishes of Antarctic waters, or northern hordes of salmon and char. Perhaps one day we will be rewarded by a companion volume to this one, depicting fishes of colder latitudes or even of the deep sea. Certainly, photographers will soon record extensive samples of the life of the entire sea, top to bottom and pole to pole, showing places and species now but imagined, by means now hardly dreamt.

There remains a plethora of challenges for writers, photographers, and scientists as the Marine Revolution proceeds. There is immense value in recording the world around us in both pictures and words, while new horizons are being discovered and before they are abused. Thus is formed a template of the past against which to measure the future. It is also important that we look beyond the fishes and into their milieu. The sea's three-dimensional texture is a mosaic of habitats to which species are exquisitely adapted and without which they cannot survive. There is much that we do not yet comprehend about species—habitat relationships in the sea, which is all the more reason to record them for later serendipity. This is to say that we should study these portraits with a deeper appreciation, beyond the pleasure they give us, towards the functions of species' forms and the character of their environments.

Books such as this one help us to care, to understand, and—hopefully—to ameliorate the impacts of humankind on the sea. Congratulations and thanks, Hillary, for making it available to us.

G. Carleton Ray
Fairbanks, Alaska

4

Preface

One day in 1969, when I was working as an editor of *Skin Diver Magazine,* Paul Tzimoulis, the publisher, came into my office with some photographs of fishes. He wondered out loud how we might make the best use of the material, and eventually we decided on doing a monthly feature on fishes. Paul designated me to write the descriptions for the lay, or non-scientific, diver. We called the feature the Fish of the Month.

Our subjects were mainly Caribbean fishes in those early days, but over the years the series expanded into the oceans of Hawaii, Australia, British Columbia, California, and other areas of the world. As more and more divers turned to underwater photography as a substitute for spearfishing, and as cameras became better and films improved, more photographs were submitted to the series and many of them were strikingly beautiful. Furthermore, they were fast making up the best collection of fish photographs to be found anywhere.

Our first attempts at fish writing were mainly comical, and included such anthropomorphic statements as "Mr. Longtail Filefish does such and such. . . ." On many occasions there were scientific mistakes, and there were times when we even went to press with the wrong identifications of fishes. But something interesting began to happen. Educated ichthyologists with years of learning and experience began to write, helping out with identifications, kindly pointing out errors, and providing their papers for reference material. Help poured in from scientists affiliated with such institutions as the Bishop Museum in Hawaii; the Smithsonian Institution; the Steinhart Aquarium; the University of California at Berkeley, San Diego, and Santa Barbara; and other universities around the world. Many of these scientists willingly looked at slides and sent back identifications. Sometimes they even corresponded among themselves when an identification remained elusive.

In 1974 an idea arose for collecting the Fish of the Month articles into a book, and Erv Rosen of Petersen Publishing Company began to explore with me the ways we might bring this idea to fruition. The letters between us on the subject filled up drawers, since we corresponded about the idea for eight years. Finally, Herb Taylor came along, recognizing that such a book might fill the gap between heavily scientific literature, full of gill raker counts and millimetric measurements of preopercular spines, and the simplified captions that appeared in so many periodicals.

As Herb Taylor began to think of how the book text would best suit the new purpose, the run-in format used in *Skin Diver* was dropped in favor of simple columns with text headings. Readers familiar with the Fish of the Month series may feel like they are not looking at the same material at all, but they are; except for numerous corrections that have been incorporated into the text, the treatment of the ichthyological information remains much the same.

In revising and updating the material for this book, I was at first embarrassed at the number of errors that were made over the years, but I gradually began to realize that even today ichthyology is changing so rapidly that the most educated scientists must work hard to keep up with new names and classifications.

The sea is still our newest frontier, and while some general observations of fishes had been made for hundreds of years, it was only with the advent of diving equipment in the 1940s that close-up, detailed observations could be made. Thus, as scientists have continued their undersea explorations in previously unexplored oceans, new observations and updating of scientific literature has taken place. It is tedious work to count gill rakers and study the stomach contents of fishes, but were it not for the efforts of dedicated ichthyologists the world over, none of us would ever fully understand or appreciate the wonders of the fish world.

— Hillary Hauser

Introduction

When Nature set about the serious business of establishing the heaven and the earth, he or she must have been in the most playful of moods when it came to the fishes of the sea. A bright pink fish here, a brilliant indigo-blue and white-striped fish there; here a purple fish with a black head, and there a brilliant yellow fish with an elongated snout. Fishes that walk on foot-like fins, fishes that spin cocoons around themselves at night, fishes that grunt, fishes that seem to kiss—all of them expressing, in their own small ways, the miracle of Nature.

And yet there is order in the fish world. Some color patterns serve for camouflage. A few are warning colorations to advertise sharp and venomous spines or distasteful qualities. Many serve for species recognition so that a fish may find a mate at spawning time. The elongated snouts help the fishes that have them to pick out tiny animals from narrow cracks and crevices in the reef. Order is expressed, too, in the scientific groupings of the fishes themselves. While it may seen that the almost 19,000 living species of fishes in existence are scattered willy-nilly throughout the oceans of the world in a fashion incomprehensible to the average person on the street, this is not so. Scientific divisions into families, genera, and species for the most part separate out the fishes that look alike and act alike, and what one learns about a certain fish in one ocean of the world can be applied to another fish in another ocean. Fish families are consistent. Therefore, a damselfish (family Pomacentridae) found in the Indo-Pacific will have similar characteristics to a damselfish found off California: pugnosed profiles, feisty, territorial behavior, with the juveniles often having bright iridescent blue spots. That fishes from widely different oceans can be so similar has been attributed to the geologic history of the world itself. Approximately 300—400 million years ago, there was one large land mass, Gondwanaland, surrounded by a world-encircling ocean. As the giant land-mass began to separate into the continents we know today, the marine animals that were distributed over a wide range became isolated and began to evolve into their own distinct forms.

The names of fishes are important in their identification and classification. Those long, tongue-twisting Latin names that seem impossible to pronounce are important tools in establishing order among the species. Taking a close look at the Latin words, we see that they often describe the fishes—either by reference to some physical characteristic, or to the way they act. Consider the name *Chaetodon ocellatus* for the Spotfin Butterflyfish. The generic or first part of the scientific name means "bristle tooth," referring to the fine, comblike teeth of the fish, and the second part, or species name, refers to the distinct black spot on the outermost edge of the dorsal fin. Another example is the Doctorfish, *Acanthurus chirurgus*. *Acanthurus* means "tail spine," and *chirurgus* is a Latin term describing an operating physician, or surgeon. *Aluterus* means "leather," and *scriptus* means "written"; *Aluterus scriptus* is the scientific name for the Scrawled Filefish, a fish that has a tough, shagreen hide and scribbled color pattern. The common names of fishes vary according to locality, and are therefore not as reliable as the Latin names. There is only one valid scientific name for every species of organism on our planet—the first one proposed with a proper description. Some scientists have named a plant or animal a second time without realizing that it had been named before. Such a name is called a synonym and is not valid. Ichthyologists are still sorting out synonyms of many species of fishes.

The names of the fishes that appear in this book, and the order in which they are presented, are based upon the Linnaean system of classification. Fishes are divided into two classes: the cartilaginous fishes, Chondrichthyes, and the bony fishes, Osteichthyes. Chondrichthyes, which includes the sharks, rays, skates, and a small, deep-water group called the chimaeras, is by far the more ancient of the two classes. Because of space limitations, examples of Chondrichthyes have not been included in this book.

The class Osteichthyes ("bony fishes") is characterized by a skeleton of bone, as compared to the cartilaginous skeletons of sharks and rays. The bony fishes have a number of common physical characteristics, including skulls with a complex system of bones, gill openings on each side covered with a bony flap (operculum), usually bony scales that overlap like shingles on a roof, and paired fins that are supported by bony rays.

Osteichthyes is divided into two subclasses: Choanichthyes (lobe-fin fishes) and Actinopterygii (ray-fin fishes). The latter subclass is divided into three superorders: Chondrostei, Holostei, and Teleostei. The first two superorders exist now largely in fossil form only, while the Teleostei ("complete bone") constitute about 96 percent of the almost 19,000 living species of fishes. All of the fishes in this book are teleosts.

Identification of bony fishes is primarily by external anatomy, including body length and depth, fin-ray counts, scale counts, tooth structure, and number of gill rakers. Often the coloration and color pattern may be used to identify a species, but many fishes have the ability to change their color patterns to match their immediate backgrounds, and sometimes the coloration of individuals within a particular species will be radically variable depending upon sex, age, and diet.

Fishes range in size from one species of Indian Ocean goby only a half-inch long to the enormous whale shark measuring 45–50 feet long, yet all of them share many common characteristics:

Respiration. Fishes take water through the mouth, strain it through gill rakers (which are like brushes) to take out particles, then pass it through gill arches and the gills themselves—feathery filaments which are lined with tiny blood vessels. The blood vessels absorb dissolved oxygen.

Scales. The scales of fishes vary in size from very large (Tarpon) to microscopic (some eels), or they are entirely absent. Generally, they are semi-transparent, like fingernails that grow out of the skin, usually overlapping like shingles on a roof. Scales may reveal growth and age like rings on a tree, particularly in temperate seas where the rate of growth varies greatly with the water temperature.

Senses. Fishes see (with eyes that function independently of each other and have no eyelids) and some, at least, react to color. They also have a sense of taste and are very sensitive to touch. Some fishes have a very sharp sense of smell, which they use to track down their prey. The lateral line of a fish, which extends the length of the body, provides a sixth sense—a combination of hearing and touch. The sensitive nerves along the lateral line pick up low-frequency sound. Thus the lateral line enables a fish to sense when it may be about to run into an object (as at night or in turbid water)—from reflection of the vibrations the fish's movement makes on the object—or when an onrushing predator is present.

Sleep. At night many fishes enter into a state of torpor that appears to be equivalent to mammalian sleep. Some can be touched or even gently handled at this time. Some parrotfishes spin mucous cocoons around themselves at night. Triggerfishes tuck themselves into a crack in the reef. Other fishes are nocturnal, staying hidden in dark caves during the day and spreading out over the reefs to feed at night. Among the nighttime feeders are squirrelfishes (Holocentridae), which have big eyes that enable them to see when the level of illumination is very low.

Color. The skin that anchors the scales to the bodies of fishes contain pigments or color cells, and fishes can expand or contract the color cells to match their environment. Other color changes, particularly of blues, involve a physical change in the surface of the skin. Some fishes can change their colors instantly and often; others never change at all. The fishes that have the ability to change colors quickly may rely on such camouflage to protect themselves against predators or, conversely, to hide their presence from unsuspecting prey. Other color changes occur with changes in emotional states: a fish becoming aggressive may darken appreciably. Often there are changes in color during courtship and spawning. The colors of some fishes, such as many of the wrasses and parrotfishes, indicate differences in sex.

These are only a few examples of the physiological wonders of fishes—enough, it is hoped, to give the reader an idea of how magical the underwater world really is. In a world where order is expressed in such variety, we are fortunate, indeed, to understand even a little of how this order works.

Tarpons & Ladyfishes

(Family Elopidae)

Tarpon

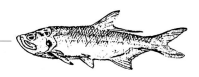

(Megalops atlanticus)

general remarks

Elopids are among the most primitive of teleost fishes. They belong to the subclass teleostei, with ventral fins on the belly and no spines in the fins. Other teleosts of the primitive type are the herrings and salmons. The Tarpon is further classed under the order Clupeiformes, which includes the herringlike fishes, and it is believed that all the rest of the bony fishes descended from this. The Elopidae includes the tarpons and ladyfishes—both of them large, strong, silvery fishes popular with anglers. The Tarpon, in particular, is one of the most sought-after game fishes in the world. It can grow to more than 8 feet and 350 pounds, and when hooked, it can leap as high as 8 or 10 feet out of the water. *Megalops* comes from two Greek words that mean "large eye," which describes a physical characteristic of the fish.

photo by Paul Humann
Photo taken in 25 feet of water on Tarpon Alley, off Grand Cayman Island, British West Indies. Humann used a Nikonos II camera with a Seacor 21mm lens, Subsea strobe, and Kodachrome film. Shot at f/8 at 1/60 second.

range and habits

The Tarpon is widely distributed on both sides of the Atlantic, and in the western Atlantic it is found from Cape Cod to Brazil, in the Caribbean, off Florida, and in the Gulf of Mexico. The fish will migrate as far north as Nova Scotia, but only during the warm months, since it prefers warm, tropical waters such as the bights of Andros, Great Bahama Bank, or Bimini. Tarpons can live in both salt and fresh water—in warm, shallow coastal areas, mangroves, estuaries, rivers, and canals—and in very stagnant, brackish water. They can do this because their swim bladders have an open connection with the gullet and are modified for taking in air. Fishermen can spot the Tarpon as it rolls at the surface to breathe.

life cycle and diet

The Tarpon spawns far offshore, or at least where currents can sweep the eggs out to sea. The females have many eggs; one individual weighing 142 pounds contained about 12 million of them. The late larval stage is called the leptocephalus, in which their bodies are ribbonlike, transparent or translucent, like the eels. In this stage they do not resemble the adults at all, except for the characteristic forked tail (the leptocephali of the eels have rounded tails). In the larval phase the Tarpon drifts to shallow marshes, mangrove swamps, or ponds, and then begins its metamorphosis into a juvenile. The juvenile Tarpon eats copepods, aquatic insects, and small fishes. The adults feed primarily on crustaceans and fishes, the grunionlike silversides being their major prey. Tarpons have been known to swim into a school of small fishes and attack simultaneously side by side, which is believed to increase the efficiency of their feeding (Randall), but more often they feed in shallow bays at night.

physical characteristics

A jutting lower jaw, turned-down mouth, and large eyes are all physical characteristics of the Tarpon. The brilliant silver body has large scales and a prolonged dorsal ray—a stout filament which extends just above the back of the fish.

Lizardfishes

(Family Synodontidae)

Sand Diver

(Synodus intermedius)

general remarks

The lizardfishes look like undersea replicas of their terrestrial namesakes. They sit on the bottom, propped up on their ventral fins in an ever-alert pose as they await their prey.

family and physical characteristics

The Sand Diver is a member of the lizardfishes (Synodontidae) and has the characteristic scaly, lizardlike head. The body is cylindrical and long and is marked with diamond-shaped blotches. There is a blackish blotch on the shoulder girdle that is hidden by the gill cover, the most distinguishing feature. Lizardfishes of the same species can vary greatly in appearance depending upon their environment.

Sand Divers found in areas of shallow, clear water and white sand bottoms will have rather faint color patterns, and those found in murky water or over darker bottoms will be more distinctly marked (Böhlke & Chaplin). Because the Sand Diver has the ability to blend into its surroundings, it is well camouflaged most of the time.

range and habits

The Sand Diver occurs on both sides of the Atlantic. In the west Atlantic it is found from Bermuda, the Bahamas, and the Carolinas to Brazil, including the Gulf of Mexico (Böhlke & Chaplin). In the West Indies the Sand Diver is the most common of the lizardfishes. It is most often seen sitting in relatively shallow water (30 feet or less) and usually stays on sand. Sometimes it is seen on reefs and rocks, but in

either case it usually rests on the bottom, swimming only occasionally. Often all that can be seen of this fish are its eyes poking up out of the sand. When the Sand Diver makes a sudden rush at its prey, it uses its tail for extra speed. When a small fish ventures near, the lizardfish darts out with lightning speed and seizes its prey with its sharp teeth. It can move so quickly that often the whole motion goes entirely unnoticed by a diver watching the action.

diet and life cycle

The Sand Diver is a voracious carnivore, as its teeth might imply. It feeds primarily on small fishes (basslets, grunts, silversides, herrings, and sardines), but it also takes in fair amounts of squid and shrimp (Randall). The Sand Diver has been known to grow to 18 inches, but most are smaller. The juveniles look much like the adults, but during the post-larval phase they look entirely different—scaleless and transparent. Still, they have the dark blotches characteristic of the species.

photo by Carl Roessler

Photo taken in 30 feet of water off the island of Bonaire. Roessler used a Nikon F camera with a 55mm lens, a Bauer strobe, and Kodachrome 25 film. Shot at 1/60 second at f/8, 2 feet from the subject.

Moray Eels

(Family Muraenidae)

California Moray

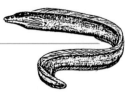

(Gymnothorax mordax)

general remarks

Marine eels are much maligned, but they are hardly as ferocious as they are made out to be. In fact, the California Moray is rather bashful, even though the species name, *mordax*, means "prone to bite." Perhaps its undeserved reputation is due to the fact that as it breathes, its mouth opens and closes regularly to reveal numerous sharp teeth. This eel is actually quite shy and remains hidden in crevices of the reef by day, venturing out to feed only at night.

family and range

The California Moray belongs to the Muraenidae, included in the Order Anguilliformes (the true eels). Muraenids are found in rock and reef areas around the world, with at least ten species in the Bahamas and one in California. The California Moray ranges from Point Conception to Magdalena Bay in Baja California. It is most common in kelp beds and rocks down to 130 feet.

physical characteristics

The California Moray has an extremely long, slender body that grows to as long as 5 feet. It is dark brown or greenish with numerous white spots. The skin of all eels is leathery and scaleless, and the body has no pectoral or pelvic fins (*gymnothorax* means "naked breast"). Muraenids have small, round gill openings. Scientists separate them from other eel families by certain aspects of their teeth and nostrils.

diet

By day the moray stays in its lair, coming out at night to feed on shrimp, octopus, mussels, and clams. If a diver drops an abalone, the moray likely will come out of hiding and tear into it. Morays are also known to get into lobster traps, most often at night.

history and life cycle

The Muraenids have a long history; moray teeth have been found in Indian middens along the coast of California, and they have also been unearthed in one Pleistocene deposit estimated to be nearly two million years old. The animals themselves live to ripe old age. Two individuals survived in an aquarium at Scripps Institution for 27 years. Young morays about a foot long have a lot of yellow on their skin, but by the time they reach 2 or 3 feet in length—the adult size—they are green. The prejuvenile muraenids go through a pelagic larval period called the leptocephalus stage. These are transparent, ribbon-like forms which float in the open ocean currents until they settle on reefs and grow into recognizable juveniles.

photo by Howard Hall
Photo was shot in 30 feet of water off Los Coronados Islands, Mexico. Hall used a Nikon F-2 with a 55mm lens in an Oceanic housing and two SR2000 strobes. Shot at ASA 64 at f/11, 1/60 second, 12 inches from the subject.

Trumpetfishes

(Family Aulostomidae)

Trumpetfish

(Aulostomus maculatus)

general remarks

The strange shape of the thin, elongated body, the long snout with the wide mouth, and the habit of drifting at odd angles all add up to a strange fish of west Atlantic seas. The body shape of the Trumpetfish actually plays a large part in its survival, for when alarmed or threatened, it will swim into an up-and-down vertical position and conceal itself next to gorgonians, sea whips, or floating sargassum. It also has been known to align itself with other larger fishes in an effort to approach unsuspecting prey.

family and physical characteristics

The Trumpetfish is a member of the Aulostomidae, which contains only three species. The family is circumtropical and is closely allied to the pipefishes, seahorses, and cornetfishes, which are elongated, unusual fishes, but trumpetfishes are distinguished by scales and a series of separate spines in front of the second dorsal fin. *Aulostomus* comes from the Greek, meaning "tube mouth," referring to the distinctive snout of the fish. The Trumpetfish is basically brown to reddish brown, and there is a yellow phase (Randall). There are horizontal, pale silver lines and a sprinkling of small black dots over its body. (*Maculatus* comes from the Latin for "spotted.") At the end of the long tubular snout is a barbel, or feeler, on the lower jaw. The anal fins and the second dorsal are symmetrically shaped and are striped at the front and colorless toward the back.

range and diet

The Trumpetfish is relatively common and has been recorded in the waters of Bermuda, Florida, the West Indies, the Bahamas, and the Gulf of Mexico (Böhlke & Chaplin). It is a voracious predator, feeding most heavily on small fishes such as blennies, grunts, squirrelfishes, and small damselfishes (Randall), as well as on shrimps. Trumpetfishes have been observed hovering vertically in the water over their prey, darting down quickly to attack. While it would seem impossible that a fish could disappear down the long, thin gullet of the Trumpetfish, the narrow snout makes room through the distensible membrane of the mouth region. The fish grows to 3 feet in length, but average size is about 2 feet. When trumpetfishes are small, they resemble the equally odd pipefishes, but pipefishes have body rings. Cornetfishes have long tubular snouts, but the snouts are much longer than the snouts of trumpetfishes. Cornetfishes also have depressed instead of compressed bodies and a long median caudal filament (Randall). Cornetfishes swim in normal fashion. When stalking its prey or hiding, the Trumpetfish will hang motionless or slowly drift to a nearby coral. While it hopes it isn't being noticed, the diver can get quite close to take a picture of this strange fish.

photo by Jack McKenney

Photo was taken in 25 feet of water off Freeport, Grand Bahama Island. McKenney used a Rolleimarin with Ektachrome X film and a No. 5B bulb. Shot at 1/125 second at f/11 at a distance of 4 feet from the subject.

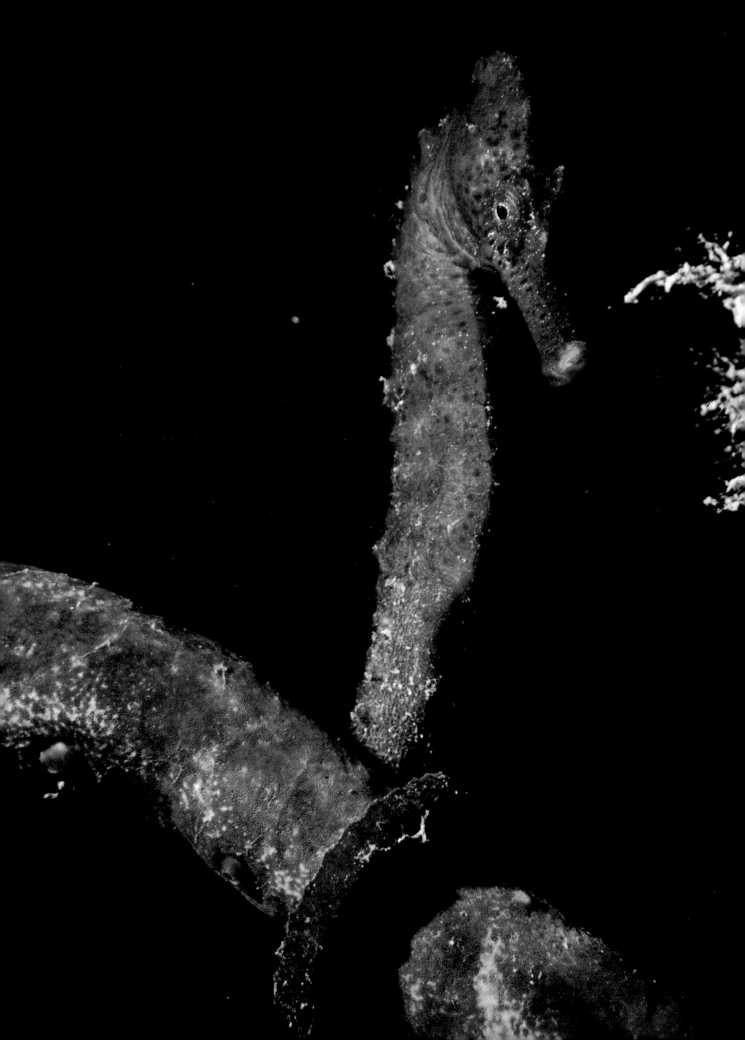

Pipefishes & Seahorses

(Family Syngnathidae)

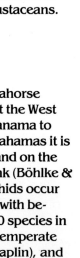

Longsnout seahorse

(Hippocampus reidi)

general remarks

Hippocampus comes from the Greek, meaning "bent horse," and it is a suitable scientific title for one of the wonderful oddities of the sea. The seahorse is, in the words of Carleton Ray, a miniature submarine chess knight. It belongs to the fish family Syngnathidae, which includes the long, almost threadlike pipefishes and the *Amphelik-turus,* the intermediate between the two groups that combines features of both. Both pipefishes and seahorses have bodies and tails that are encased in a bony armorlike shell and long tubular snouts with tiny mouths at the end. They have no spinous dorsal or ventral fins. However, where the bodies of the pipefishes are straight, seahorses have heads that are bent sharply down and prehensile tails that are capable of wrapping around seagrasses and corals. With this device the animals can anchor themselves to something solid, thereby

avoiding being dashed about in ocean currents. Pipefishes swim horizontally, like most fishes, whereas seahorses swim with their bodies straight up and down. This swimming is not very efficient, since seahorses have no tail fins, and any locomotion is accomplished by a rapid fluttering of the dorsal and pectoral fins.

family and physical characteristics

The Longsnout Seahorse is one of three seahorse species found in the Caribbean. It is the largest of the three, growing to 4 or 5 inches in length (6 inches if the tail is uncoiled). It is distinguished from the Bahaman Seahorse *(Hippo-campus erectus)* by its color pattern—dark spots on a lighter background. The Longsnout Seahorse also has a longer snout (Böhlke & Chaplin) and a more slender body (Randall). The coloration of this seahorse, although highly variable, may include whitish bands, or partial bands, on the trunk and tail, in addition to the round black dots. The Longsnout Seahorse also has a well-developed coronet, the crown on top of the head.

breeding and diet

The breeding habits of seahorses are as strange as the animals themselves. The female deposits the eggs, which can number up to a few hundred, in a pouch on the male's belly, where they incubate. After about six weeks they hatch, often after the male rubs his pouch against some undersea object to hasten the birth. There can be 100 or more perfectly formed young seahorses at one hatching, each one about $5/8$ inch long. They swim away from their parents to begin feeding almost immediately on live food, primarily planktonic crustaceans. The seahorse is carnivorous, and the adults feed mainly on crustaceans.

range

The Longsnout Seahorse ranges throughout the West Indies and from Panama to Bermuda. In the Bahamas it is found off Nassau and on the Great Bahama Bank (Böhlke & Chaplin). Syngnathids occur around the world, with between 150 and 200 species in both tropical and temperate seas (Böhlke & Chaplin), and with individuals measuring from less than an inch to a foot in length.

photo by Carl Roessler
Photo was taken in 20 feet of water at Frederiksted Pier, St. Croix, U.S. Virgin Islands. Roessler used a Nikon F in a Nikomar housing with a 55mm lens and a Bauer E252 strobe. Shot at f/11, 15 inches from the subject.

Batfishes

(Family Ogcocephalidae)

Galapagos Batfish

(Ogcocephalus darwini)

general remarks

Bizarre, strange, grotesque—this is the odd batfish, a fish that really doesn't behave at all like a fish. Instead of swimming in the normal fashion, the batfish uses its pectoral fins to walk around on the bottom. If danger presents itself, the batfish will try to swim, but at best this is awkward and slow. Usually the batfish will stay in one spot and try to camouflage itself. From time to time it will prop itself up on the strong pectoral fins to look around. The batfish is also unusual in that it fishes for its meals just like the frogfishes. It does this with the antenna-like fishing pole at the top of its head, which is tipped with a baitlike lure. The fish wiggles this around to attract small fishes, and since it is usually successfully camouflaged, the unwary prey easily comes in close enough for the batfish to leap into action.

range and family

The Galapagos Batfish (*O. darwini*), with its characteristic

photo by Carl Roessler
Photo taken in 40 feet of water in Bartholomew Bay in the Galapagos. Roessler used a Nikon F camera with a 24mm lens, Subsea strobe, and Kodachrome II film. Shot at 1/60 second at f/11, 15 inches from the subject.
drawing: Top view.

red lips and white pectoral fins, is found only in the Galapagos Islands. According to Dr. Richard Rosenblatt, curator of marine vertebrates at Scripps, *O. darwini* was named only recently, in 1959. The Galapagos Batfish is a member of the Ogcocephalidae family, which is included under the order Lophiiformes, as are the frogfishes (Antennariidae) and deep-sea anglerfishes. These batfishes are not to be confused with the batfishes that have the long batlike fins and are included with the spadefishes in the Ephippidae. The ogcocephalids are tough and scaleless, and their broad, flattened bodies are covered with tubercles and spines which camouflage them effectively against the bottom. The word *ogcocephalid* comes from Greek words meaning "hook head." In the batfishes the fishing pole is actually the first dorsal spine placed in a depression between the snout tip and the mouth. In the frogfishes the antenna is on the top of the snout. The late Steinhart ichthyologist Earl Herald said that he observed some batfishes wiggling the lure to the right, with others vibrating it to the left. Other ichthyologists have said that the lure of the batfish works up and down, like a piston.

diet and habits

Batfishes eat small fishes, mollusks, crustaceans, and worms. They sit on shallow, sandy bottoms, sometimes in less than 10 feet of water, and because of their camouflage they are relatively difficult to spot. Some divers have seen batfishes actually throwing sand over themselves in an effort to hide, and sometimes they won't move from this hiding place unless they are prodded. The Galapagos Batfish grows to about 6 inches in length. While its tough, bony hide makes it an undesirable fish for commercial purposes, it is often captured by bottom trawls. Some batfishes have been kept in aquariums, but as soon as small fishes are introduced into a tank with them, they are known to begin fishing.

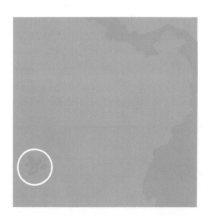

Squirrelfishes & Soldierfishes

(Family Holocentridae)

Squirrelfishes and soldierfishes are the subaqueous night owls of the reef. By day they hang in sleepy suspension under a protective rock or coral overhang, drifting back and forth with the currents. At night they come alive and spread out over the reef in search of food. Studies of the feeding habits of these fishes reinforce this fact, because individuals collected at night and during early morning hours invariably have some sort of food in their stomachs, whereas specimens collected during the day are usually empty.

Red color and big eyes are characteristics of most members of the Holocentridae family of squirrelfishes and soldierfishes. It has been speculated that the big eyes of these fishes evolved from their living in the dark. The red coloration and big eyes are also common among the bigeyes (Family Priacanthidae) and the cardinalfishes (Family Apogonidae), two groups of fishes that also forage at night and hide by day under ledges in the reef.

Another characteristic of the holocentrids is an abundance of serrated, spiny scales and stout, sharp spines. Ichthyologists differentiate between the subfamilies of the Holocentridae by taking a close look at the spine structures of the fishes.

Holocentrids are divided into two subfamilies: Holocentrinae (squirrelfishes) and Myripristinae (soldierfishes); the chief difference between the two is that the squirrelfishes have a long, sharp preopercular spine (on the cheek), while the soldierfishes do not. Also, soldierfishes are more snub-nosed than squirrelfishes and usually have some sort of darkened bar or similar marking at the edge of the gill cover. Squirrelfishes often appear more striped than soldierfishes, too.

Until recently the Holocentridae contained only the genus *Holocentrus*. However, when two Atlantic species of *Holocentrus* were found to have an extension of the air bladder reaching the skull (Randall), two additional genera were differentiated: *Flammeo* and *Adioryx*. The Myripristinae includes the genera *Myripristis*, *Ostichthys*, *Plectrypops*, and *Corniger*.

In some squirrelfishes the connection between the swim bladder and the auditory part of the skull is believed to increase hearing ability (Böhlke &

Chaplin), and the swim bladder may also serve as a sound box for the noise that some species of squirrelfishes make.

There are less than 100 species of Holocentridae worldwide, and where they are found they exhibit the same physical characteristics (red and spiny) and the same behavioral characteristics (hiding by day and feeding at night). In Hawaii the squirrelfishes are called "ala'ihi," and the soldierfishes "menpachis" or "'u'us." In the Spanish-speaking Gulf of California squirrelfishes are called "Pesces ardilla" and soldierfishes "soldados." There are nine species of holocentrids distributed among five genera in the West Indies.

The squirrelfishes and soldierfishes are highly regarded food fishes, but because they are small, spiny, and difficult to handle, they have little commercial value. The largest holocentrids are between 1 and 2 feet in length.

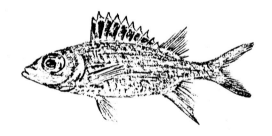

Spotfin Squirrelfish (*Flammeo sammara*)

photo by John Randall

Photo was taken in 8 feet of water at Eniwetok Atoll, Marshall Islands. Randall used a Nikonos, Hydro Photo close-up lens, Honeywell Strobonar and Ektachrome X film. Shot at 1/60 second at f/22, 15 inches from the subject.

Squirrelfish

(Holocentrus rufus)

general remarks

Holocentrus comes from the Greek, meaning "spinous all over," and *rufus* comes from the Latin, meaning "red." These terms describe in part the holocentrid that is commonly called Squirrelfish. Sometimes it is called Longspine Squirrelfish, but this name is more often used for *Flammeo marianus,* another type of holocentrid.

physical characteristics

Squirrelfishes are generally red and spiny; *H. rufus* has a series of white spots or triangles on the dorsal fin membranes near the tips of the dorsal spines. The fish looks very similar to *H. ascensionis,* the Longjaw Squirrelfish, but the difference between the two is that this dorsal fin area in *H. ascensionis* is undifferentiated in color. The Squirrelfish is red overall, with alternating red and white bands running its vertical length. There is a white bar below the eye and a vertical white bar along the edge of the preopercle (front part of the gill cover). There is one long sharp spine at the angle of the preopercle, which can cause a toxic reaction in humans. The scales are razor-sharp, and the white-tipped spines of the dorsal are veritable needles. Experienced fishermen rarely handle the Squirrelfish with bare hands. *H. rufus* and *H. ascensionis* are so similar that in the past they were not separated. *H. ascensionis* tends to be more abundant on offshore patch reefs (Böhlke & Chaplin). Both species of *Holocentrus* share a similar characteristic of the caudal fin, in that the upper lobe is much longer than the lower lobe.

growth cycle and habits

The juvenile post-larval Squirrelfishes are long and silvery in appearance, much different from the adults. They are so different from the adult in appearance that for a time they were believed to be a separate genus, *Rhynchichthys,* and ichthyologists today often refer to the postlarval phase of squirrelfishes as the "rhynchichthys stage." They drift in the open ocean currents, feeding on plankton, and are often preyed upon by larger fishes such as tuna. Like many larval fishes, the juvenile has a series of spines on its head, which possibly helps in flotation or in protection from predators. The spines gradually diminish with age, and as the young fish begins to adopt the adult characteristics, it settles out of the plankton currents to assume the adult lifestyle—hiding by day under rocks and ledges in big groups, and foraging alone along the reefs when the sun goes down. The maximum length of the Squirrelfish is about 12 inches.

diet

The diet of the adult Squirrelfish consists largely of crustaceans such as crabs and shrimps (including mysids), but it also eats gastropods, ophiuroids, and polychaetes (Randall). The small teeth of the Squirrelfish are thought to be why it rarely eats smaller fishes.

range

The Squirrelfish ranges from Bermuda, the Bahamas, and the Carolinas to the lesser Antilles, including the Central American coast (Böhlke & Chaplin). It is a common fish on the coral reefs within its range, and it lives in depths from the shoreline down to about 100 feet.

photo by Jack McKenney
Photo was taken in 55 feet of water on the deep reef off Freeport, Grand Bahama Island. McKenney used a Rolleimarin with a No. 1 closeup lens, No. 5B bulb, and Ektachrome X film. Shot at 1/125 second at f/22.

Blackbar Soldierfish

(Myripristis jacobus)

general remarks and physical characteristics

Soldierfishes are more snub-nosed than the squirrelfishes, and make up the subfamily Myripristinae within the Holocentridae. In the Atlantic the Blackbar Soliderfish is the only species of Myripristinae, and it is perhaps one of the most easily identified of the soldierfishes. There is a prom-inent dark bar just behind the head along the gill cover. This bar can be black or dark red, but it is always evident. The color of the bar, as well as the overall red color of the fish, often varies in intensity, in-fluenced by factors such as en-vironment or time of day. The dorsal spines of the fish are tipped in white, and the edges of the other fins are rimmed in white. While squirrelfishes of the genus *Holocentrus* have well-developed preopercular spines, soldierfishes do not. Even so, this is still a spiny, sharp-scaled fish. *Myripristis* comes from the two Greek words meaning "myriad" and "saw" and refers to the many sawlike spines of the sol-dierfish.

growth cycle and range

Like the squirrelfishes, young soldierfishes go through a postlarval, planktonic phase in which they drift about over a wide area of open ocean. Dur-ing this period the fish is elon-gated and silvery, having many spines about the head and a spine in front of the snout. The open-ocean float-ing period subjects the fishes to a wide dispersal, and by the time they settle down to an adult life on the reef, they are often settling a great distance away from where they were hatched. The Blackbar Sol-dierfish is found on both sides of the Atlantic, in the western Atlantic from northern Florida to Brazil. In the Bahamas it is found in the waters of the Little Bahamas and Great Bahama Banks and Hogsty Reef. It is also found throughout the Gulf of Mexico (Böhlke & Chaplin).

habits

Like squirrelfishes, soldier-fishes spend their daylight hours in the dark of underwa-ter ledges or at the back of caves, and only on occasion during the day will the Black-bar Soldierfish make short dashes from one hole to another. Böhlke and Chaplin describe this species as having "more often than not" a parasi-tic isopod fastened between the eyes—the crustacean oriented in the same direction as the fish.

diet

While most holocentrids eat crustaceans (crabs and shrimp), the Blackbar Sol-dierfish feeds predominantly on planktonic organisms. This includes the larvae of crabs and shrimps, stomatopod lar-vae, mysids, polychaete worms, fish larvae, amphi-pods, copepods, isopods, and the larvae of cephalopods and hermit crabs (Randall). The Blackbar Soldierfish would be a good food fish were it not for its small size (8 inches max-imum).

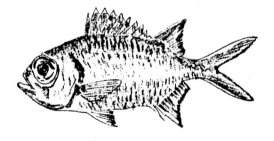

photo by Jack McKenney
Photo taken in 50 feet of water off St. Croix, U.S. Virgin Islands. McKenney used a Rol-leimarin, No. 2 close-up lens, Honeywell strobe in an Ikelite housing, and Ektachrome X film. Shot at 1/125 second at f/11.

Barracudas

(Family Sphyraenidae

Great Barracuda

(Sphyraena barracuda

general remarks

Often a diver may get the feeling that extra eyes are watching him as he explores a reef, and often when that happens it is because there is a barracuda nearby. The barracuda, looking like an underwater missile with fangs, is a curious fish that waits and watches. It is not as dangerous as it is made out to be. Ichthyologists have noted only 30 reported attacks involving barracudas, and almost all of them were either in murky water (where the barracuda mistakenly figured a swimmer's limb for a fish in trouble), or when a flashing object was mistaken for a wounded fish, or when the barracuda was provoked. Other situations that can induce attack are fast, sudden, or irregular movements in the water, or splashing on the surface (especially in murky conditions). Spearing fish or carrying wounded fish in the presence of barracudas is also inviting trouble. The advice from experts is to swim normally and avoid carrying wounded fish or wearing shiny objects (such as jewelry) in the water. Probably the barracuda's biggest menace to man is not the possibility of attack, but rather is ciguatera (fish poisoning). While young specimens up to 3 pounds have been said to be good eating, the larger barracudas have been known to cause toxic reactions. The barracudas are carnivorous, feeding mainly on fishes smaller than themselves.

range and family

There are 20 species of barracudas around the world, all members of the *Sphyraenidae*. Only three species of barracuda are found in the Caribbean, and of these three the largest is the Great Barracuda *(S. barracuda).* The other two species, called sennets, are smaller, less common, and often seen with jacks. The Great Barracuda is known to range in tropical and temperate waters around the world, except in the eastern Pacific and Mediterranean Sea. In the west Atlantic it ranges from the New England coast to southeastern Brazil, including the Gulf of Mexico (Böhlke & Chaplin).

physical characteristics

The sinister jaws, the elongated, silvery body, and the long, sharp teeth are physical characteristics associated with all of the barracuda species. The Great Barracuda is differentiated from its Caribbean relatives (*S. guachancho* and *S. picudilla)* by a lower number of lateral-line scales (Randall) and the black blotches on its lower side, which the others do not have. The Great Barracuda is always silvery with green or gray above, but the fish can change colors to match its environment. When near the ocean bottom, the Great Barracuda can show a pattern of seven bars over its body. Young barracudas (several inches in length) have a dark lateral stripe which becomes the blotched pattern as the fish matures. However, young specimens have been seen with the adult pattern. The Great Barracuda has been reported to reach 10 feet, but such length needs confirmation; it rarely exceeds 5 feet.

photo by David Doubilet
Photo taken in 20 feet of water at Trumpet Reef, off Andros Island in the Bahamas. Doubilet used a Rolleimarin SL 66, Subsea strobe, and Ektachrome Professional film. Shot at 1/30 second at f/11, 2 feet from the subject.

Scorpionfishes & Rockfishes

(Family Scorpaenidae)

The word "scorpion" creates an immediate picture of venom and stings, and scorpionfishes are aptly named for their ability to inflict painful, stinging wounds in both fish and man. These fishes have short, stout spines on the head and strong spines in the dorsal, anal, and ventral fins, which are venomous. Even without the venom, the spines of scorpionfishes can cause pain and infection, and fishermen learn to handle these fishes with care. Several Indo-Pacific species (such as the *Pterois* turkeyfishes or *Synanceia* stonefishes) are particularly venomous and can cause painful, sometimes even fatal, wounds.

All scorpionfishes are bottom-dwellers. Because these fishes lack the air bladder which regulates buoyancy, they don't swim much, making only short, quick dashes either to capture food or to escape to shelter. They are excellent camouflagers, with their blotchy bodies, often with fleshy filaments or flaps, blending almost perfectly into their surroundings. Because of their habit of lying around in rocky areas they are often called rockfishes, particularly off the California coast where the Scorpaenidae constitutes the largest family of fishes in the range.

The major characteristic feature of the Scorpaenidae is the bony plate that extends across the cheek from beneath the eye to the operculum. This bone is called the suborbital stay, and it is the reason why scorpionfishes are referred to as mail-cheeked. Usually there are spines extending from this bone, which add to the overall spiky appearance of the fish.

There are several hundred species of scorpionfishes around the world, making it one of the largest of fish families. Those which live in very deep water tend to become quite red overall. No matter where these fishes are found, they will behave in much the same manner and will exhibit similar physical characteristics. In the Gulf of California scorpionfishes are called "Peces escorpion," and in Polynesia some species are called "nohu." All of them must be handled with care, because of the treacherous spines.

The growth cycle of scorpionfishes varies. Some species are ovoviviparous, the eggs fertilized internally and hatching from the female. Others lay their eggs in mucous clusters at about the time of hatching, with the adults watching over the clusters to protect them from predators.

The rockfishes of the Pacific coast of North America are temperate-water scorpaenids, and while they may appear to be less treacherous than their tropical relatives, they still have hazardous spines. The rockfishes consist of about 61 species living in both deep and shallow water from Alaska to Baja California, with 57 species grouped together in the genus *Sebastes*. (In the past some rockfishes were grouped together under *Sebastodes*, but now they all are included in the *Sebastes*.) *Sebastes* is distinguished by having 13 dorsal fin spines and palatine teeth.

Many rockfishes are named for their physical characteristics (colors, spines, etc.), while others get their names from where they live or how they act. As with tropical scorpaenids, it is difficult for ichthyologists to distinguish between individual species of rockfishes unless they inspect gill rakers, scales, fin rays, and head spines. Brown and red are common colors for rockfishes, the ones from deep water (up to 200 fathoms) often brighter red than the shallow-water, inshore species.

Rockfishes are excellent food fish and are often called rock cod, although there is no connection whatsoever to the cod family Gadidae. All *Sebastes* rockfishes are ovoviviparous, giving birth to live young. Fertilization is internal, and the embryos develop within the female parent. One female can release as many as 2,000,000 tiny embryos at one spawning (Fitch and Lavenberg).

Kelp Rockfish (Sebastes atrovirens)

photo by Bob Evans

Photo taken in 45 feet of water off Santa Cruz Island, California. Evans used a Nikon F camera with a 55mm lens, Subsea strobe, and Ektachrome X film. Shot at 1/60 second at f/16, 12 inches from the subject.

Sailfin Leaf Fish

(Taenianotus triacanthus)

general remarks

The Sailfin Leaf Fish derives its name from its unique appearance and behavior. When alarmed, it will "play dead," rocking back and forth in the surge like a leaf. The highly compressed, thin body and large dorsal fin add to its leafy appearance. The word *taenianotus* comes from the Greek, meaning "ribbon back," which describes the big sail-like dorsal that extends from above the eye to the tail.

family

The Sailfin Leaf Fish is a tropical Indo-Pacific scorpionfish. These fishes are sometimes capable of inflicting painful wounds to a careless fisherman or diver. However, *Taenianotus* does not appear to be as hazardous as some of the other scorpionfish species such as the Lionfish or Turkeyfish, which are found within the same range. The Sailfin Leaf Fish reportedly can be handled safely by the big dorsal fin, and even within the palm of the hand. Like other scorpaenids, the Sailfin Leaf Fin has many protuberances— fleshy, weed like cirri over the eyes and around the mouth, and knobby papillae scattered over the scaleless body. These irregularities camouflage the fish against the rough terrain of the reef.

physical characteristics, range, and diet

The color of the Sailfin Leaf Fish can be red, brown, yellow, and black, with scattered blotches overall. Gosline and Brock have recorded the fish from shallow water to depths over 300 feet deep. It ranges throughout the tropical Indo-Pacific, specifically from the East Indies through Polynesia to as far as Hawaii. It has also been recorded along South Africa in the Indian Ocean. The fish is carnivorous and eats other fishes as well as shrimps and other small crustaceans. The Sailfin Leaf Fish is not large, the full-grown individual reaching only about 3 or 4 inches. Once considered to be rare, it is now believed to be more common.

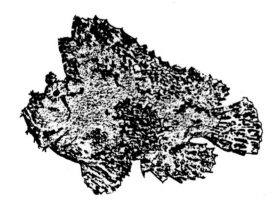

photo by Chris Newbert

Photo was taken in 135 feet of water on the Deep Reef off Kailua-Kona, Hawaii. Newbert used a Canon F1 in an Ikelite housing with a flat port, Oceanic/Farallon 2003 strobe. Shot at 1/60 second, f/16, one foot from subject.

Yelloweye Rockfish

(Sebastes ruberrimus)

range and habits

The Yelloweye Rockfish is one of 35 species of the Scorpaenidae found off British Columbia and the Gulf of Alaska. Its range extends south along the California coast to Ensenada, Mexico, where approximately 26 additional rockfish species live. It is common where found and is one of the bigger rockfishes, reaching a length of 3 feet. According to ichthyologist John L. Hart, the Yelloweye Rockfish is most often found from 60 to 90 feet, but its common range is between 150 and 1,200 feet. Like many of the rockfishes that come from deep water, the Yelloweye Rockfish is bright red. An alternative common name is Turkey Red Rockfish (Miller and Lea). Its scientific name,

Sebastes ruberrimus, comes from Greek and Latin words that mean "magnificent" and "very red." For a time the fish was called a Red Snapper, but this term is now confined to a species within the snapper family.

physical characteristics

The Yelloweye Rockfish ranges from bright red to orange yellow, sometimes washed with pink on the back and sides becoming paler below. The fins are pink, usually with black on the tips. Very large specimens, according to Hart, have black mottling around the head. The peritoneum (the lining of the abdominal cavity) is white with black dots. The eyes of the fish are yellow, and this physical characteristic is the source of the common name of the fish.

growth cycle, habits, and diet

The juvenile Yelloweye Rockfish is so different from the adult that as late as 1954 it was described as an entirely separate species, *S. bilineata.* In the young there is a light stripe along the entire lateral line to the base of the tail, where it divides at right angles to surround the caudal peduncle. A second light stripe extends below the first from ahead of the eye to below the rayed part of the dorsal fin. (This double-striped configuration is the source of the *bilineata* designation.) The Yelloweye Rockfish of the northern areas gives birth to its young in June, and in their pelagic, planktonic youth, the young eat planktonic shrimps and other microscopic animals. When the Yelloweye Rockfish reaches about 15 inches in length, the ridges on top of the head between the eyes break up into numerous low spines. The adult fish feeds on squid, octopus, crabs, small fishes, and also lingcod spawn. The Yelloweye Rockfish is very often sold as rock cod, although it is no relation to the cod family, Gadidae.

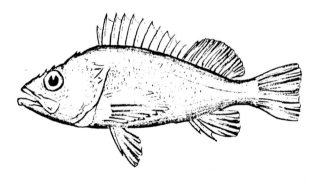

photo by Lou Lehmann

Lehmann photographed the fish in 90 feet of water off Quadra Island, Campbell River, British Columbia. He used a Nikon F and 55mm micro lens in an Ikelite housing, with an Ikelite Substrobe 150. Shot at ASA 25, 2 feet from the subject.

Groupers & Sea Basses

(Family Serranidae)

The Serranidae includes a wide variety of species with individuals ranging from a few inches to 12 feet in length, and from a few ounces to 1,000 pounds. It includes the big, friendly groupers and the small hamlets (Hypoplectrus) or the lovely little species of Anthiinae. Although the typical basslike body is said to be easy to distinguish, this can be confusing when the big outline of the Epinephelus or Mycteroperca grouper is compared to a 5- or 6-inch sea bass such as the Tobaccofish. Neither does a 1,000 pound grouper (from which stories have arisen about divers being swallowed alive) compare with the small hamlets. There are 350 to 400 species of serranids in tropical and temperate waters around the world, making it one of the largest of fish families.

The Serranidae is among the least specialized families of fishes, and therefore it is difficult to characterize by a few features. Among the more important features are a large mouth with a maxilla exposed on the cheek and bands of slender teeth in the jaws, usually with a few stout canines, and nearly always a serrate preopercle (front bone of the gill cover). Serranus comes from the Latin, meaning "saw," which refers to this last characteristic. The related soapfishes (Grammistidae), sometimes included as a subfamily of the Serranidae, are distinctive in possessing a skin toxin and in having upper borders of the gill cover attached to the body with a flap of skin.

Most serranids—especially the larger ones—are bottom-dwellers, sitting in caves or near protective ledges when they don't swim, and lazing along slowly over the bottom when they do swim. The larger ones, such as the groupers, can be more skittish than the smaller sea basses or hamlets. However, divers have easily lured big groupers close to their cameras with food or bright objects such as mirrors. Even though the smaller serranids may dart off to hide in a crack in the reef, their curiosity will often cause them to emerge a little later in some other nearby spot. All serranids are carnivorous, feeding primarily on fishes and crustaceans such as shrimps and crabs.

Serranids exhibit interesting and bizarre sexual characteristics. Some of the larger ones, such as the groupers (Epinephelus, Mycteroperca, and Cephalopholis), start out as females and change to males in later life. Parrotfishes (Scaridae) and wrasses (Labridae) also do this, with the "terminal-phase" males more brightly colored than the initial-phase individuals. Some of the smaller serranids, such as the Serranus and Hypoplectrus genera, are hermaphroditic, being male and female at the same time.

There have been a number of scientific adjustments and name changes within the Serranidae family, many of them recent. In the groupers, some ichthyologists have lumped five genera into Epinephelus, but there are other scientists who disagree with this. Therefore, the Coney remains Cephalopholis, and the Graysby, formerly Petrometopon, is now determined also to be Cephalopholis. Epinephelus and Mycteroperca comprise the larger groupers, the Cephalopholis the smaller groupers; these fishes exhibit sex reversal, starting out mature life as females and changing to males when they are larger.

The smaller Serranus (Harlequin Bass and Tobaccofish) reach lengths of only 4 inches and 7 inches, respectively, and are hermaphroditic, as are the hamlets.

The hamlets (Hypoplectrus) are deeper bodied and generally less cigar-shaped than other serranids, but they have the big serranid mouth, ctenoid scales, and like other members of the family, they are carnivorous, feeding almost exclusively on crustaceans and small fishes. While the Serranidae is represented in tropical and temperate waters around the world, the hamlets are recorded only in the western Atlantic.

We also include here the Scalefin Anthias (Anthias squamipinnis) of the Indo-Pacific, which formerly was called Goldfish and was classified by some ichthyologists in its own family, Anthiidae.

Tobaccofish (Serranus tabacarius)

photo by Chris Newbert
Photo taken in 50 feet of water off Grand Cayman Island. Newbert used a Canon F-1 with a 50mm macro lens, a Hydro 35 housing, Farallon/Oceanic 2003 strobe, and Kodachrome 25 film. Shot at f/16, 10 inches from the subject.

Nassau Grouper

(Epinephelus striatus)

general remarks

Friendly fish are the exception rather than the rule, and if a diver comes across such a fish—one that will pose for pictures, endure a pat on the head, and enjoy a hand-fed snack—the dive becomes a one-of-a-kind experience. The Nassau Grouper is a fish that will go out of its way to be friendly, and some of them become so conditioned that they will come at the sound of air bubbles from a diving tank.

physical characteristics

Of all the groupers, the Nassau Grouper is one of the most easily identified. There are irregular, vertical, dark bands on the body, and a characteristic diagonal dark band through the eye. The bands are highly changeable, ranging between brown and olive, while the background color varies among pale green, gray, or white. The colors themselves can differ in intensity, since the fish can instantly change its coloring, depending upon mood and environment. The bands are sometimes so pale that they are indistinguishable on a pale white background, and individuals in depths of 60 feet or more very often have a reddish color. When the Nassau Grouper exhibits the red coloration, it can easily be confused with the Red Grouper *(Epinephelus morio)*. *E. morio*, however, does not have the black saddle at the base of the tail, and the dorsal fin is not notched between the spines as it is on the Nassau Grouper. In spite of the radically different color phases, there are several characteristic features of the Nassau Grouper which provide the key to identification of the species. The black spots around the eyes are characteristic, and the big black spot at the base of the tail is always present. Even the juveniles, which also have the ability to change colors between pale and dark, are recognizable as the species because of these markings.

family and diet

Groupers are the larger representatives of the Serranidae family of fishes, which includes a wide variety of species ranging from a few inches to 12 feet in length. The Nassau Grouper grows to 3 or 4 feet and a maximum weight of 55 pounds. As is typical of the larger serranids, it is a relatively slow-moving, sedentary fish that can move fast when it wants to. It will stay close to the bottom or near protective shelter, but in a marine preserve its curious nature will often bring it out into the open where it may be enticed to feed from the diver's hand. As with all other serranids, the Nassau Grouper is carnivorous, feeding mainly on fishes, crustaceans (crabs, spiny lobsters), stomatopods, octopuses, and squid. The older individuals feed more on fishes and less on crustaceans (Randall).

growth cycle and range

The Nassau Grouper is a sex-changer, starting out as a female then changing over to a male in later stages. The young groupers are often found in shallow seagrass beds, while the adults stay close to the reef, often in depths less than 35 feet. The Nassau Grouper is very common in the Bahamas and is found throughout the tropical west Atlantic from Bermuda to Brazil, including the Gulf of Mexico. A few stragglers range to North Carolina (Cape Hatteras). This grouper is one of the most valued food fishes of the West Indies, which is a cruel irony, since its friendly and inquisitive nature makes it an easy target for the spearfisherman.

photo by Jack McKenney

Photo was taken in 55 feet of water off the Deep Reef, Freeport, Grand Bahamas. McKenney used a Rolleimarin camera with a No. 5 blue flash, F3.5 lens, Ektachrome X film. Shot at f/8, 1/125 second, four feet from subject.

Drawing: Dark and light phases.

Yellowfin Grouper

(Mycteroperca venenosa)

general remarks

Groupers have no intermuscular bones and are therefore one of the most desirable fishes for the table. The Yellowfin Grouper is not so popular, however, because it is sometimes known to cause ciguatera (fish poisoning) when eaten. The scientific name of the fish—*venenosa*—means "venomous" in Latin, in reference to this characteristic. The larger individuals are more apt to be toxic.

physical characteristics

The outer part of the pectoral fins of the Yellowfin Grouper are usually a bright orange-yellow, a characteristic that has given the fish its common name. Like other groupers, this species can change colors to match its surroundings, and over a sand bottom it will appear nearly white, whereas in a dark hole or cave it will appear nearly black. Its most usual color phase is an overall gray to olive with dark brown spots or blotches in irregular, horizontal rows. There are sometimes dark red or orange spots. *M. venenosa* is the most common species of *Mycteroperca* in the Bahamas and closely resembles *M. bonaci* (Black Grouper). In *M. bonaci* the dark blotches are more regularly aligned, and while the pectoral fin of *M. bonaci* is rimmed with orange, the orange margin is narrow (about one fifth the fin), whereas the yellow section of *venenosa* is broad (roughly one third the fin) (Böhlke & Chaplin).

family and growth cycle

Like other members of the Serranidae family of fishes, the Yellowfin Grouper starts out life as female and changes into a male in later life. This is one of the larger groupers of the Bahamas, growing to a maximum length of about 3 feet and a weight of 35 pounds, not quite as large as the Nassau Grouper, which grows to 55 pounds.

diet and range

The Yellowfin Grouper feeds on a wide variety of fishes which comprise at least 95 percent of its diet. Randall's studies determined that the fish preys on a variety of fishes including Sergeant Majors *(Abudefduf saxatilis)*, Trumpetfish *(Aulostomus maculatus)*, Bar Jacks *(Caranx ruber)*, surgeonfish (acanthurids), grunts (haemulids), squirrelfish (holocentrids), parrotfishes (scarids), and wrasses (labrids). The Yellowfin Grouper is found from Bermuda, through the West Indies, and off the coast of Florida to Brazil, including the Gulf of Mexico. Among the groupers it is the more active, faster swimming fish, and it has been known to rise up off the bottom to take a trolled lure. The fact that it feeds on the swift-moving Bar Jack *(Caranx ruber)* is additional evidence that the Yellowfin Grouper is capable of rapid movement.

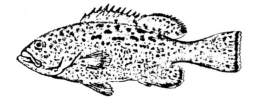

photo by Paul Tzimoulis

The photo was taken in 30 feet of water at Telephone Pole Reef, San Salvador Island, Bahamas. Tzimoulis used a Rebikoff-Alpha DR-8 U/W camera unit. Shot at f/8, 1/160 second, 3 feet from the subject with Ektachrome 64 film.

Coney

(Cephalopholis fulva)

physical characteristics

The Coney is a small grouper, one of the serranids that exhibits a spectacular range of colors. The most common color phase is a reddish brown, but there are also pale cream-colored, green, or brown phases. One common phase is sharply bicolor, with the upper part of the fish a dark color, the lower section almost white, and the dividing line at the level of the eye. The bicolor phase may be the "excitement phase," occurring when the fish is frightened or agitated over the prospects of food (Böhlke & Chaplin). However, this phase is often seen underwater (Randall). There is also a golden-yellow phase, which reportedly is "rare," but which also has commonly been seen by divers. In spite of all these variations on a color theme, there are definite markings that distinguish the Coney. These are (1) the blue, white, or black spots that always appear over the head and most of the body, blue being the most common color of the spots; (2) the two black spots on the base of the tail, one behind the other; and (3) the two dark spots on the lower lip (faint in our pictured specimen). These markings are found on all Coneys, no matter what their overall color.

range and habits

Whether the color variations are caused by environment, the process of aging, or other factors is not fully known by ichthyologists, but it is known that Coney individuals found in deeper water are generally more red than those found in shallower inshore areas. The Coney is found from depths of a few feet to 500 feet and is quite common throughout the tropical west Atlantic (primarily the West Indies), off Bermuda, and from southern Florida to southeast Brazil, including the Gulf of Mexico. The fish generally stays close to the bottom, cruising the reefs in search of crustaceans and fish. The Coney grows to 1 foot, which is small in comparison to its larger grouper relatives. It is a good food fish and is commonly caught on hook and line, but underwater it is rather unfriendly and difficult to approach.

photo by Carl Roessler

Photo was taken in 50 feet of water off Curacao, Netherlands Antilles. Roessler used a Nikon F camera with a 55mm lens, a Hydro strobe, Kodachrome II film. Shot at 1/60 second at f/11, 18 inches from subject.

Drawing: Bicolor phase

Graysby

(Cephalopholis cruentata)

general remarks

Recent investigations by ichthyologists into a number of species within the Serranidae have led to different generic names. The Graysby, formerly *Petrometopon* (from the Greek words meaning "stone" and "forehead"), is now included with the Coney in the genus *Cephalopholis* ("scale head").

physical characteristics

The Graysby is a tropical western Atlantic grouper that reaches only about 1 foot in length. The most distinguishing characteristic of the fish is the three (sometimes four) black spots below the dorsal fin, but since the Graysby, like other serranids, can alter its colors considerably to match its immediate environment, these spots are sometimes white. The overall ground color appears red because of the numerous red or red-brown spots on a white background. *Cruentata* comes from the Latin, meaning "dyed with blood," which refers to the red coloration of the fish. The red spots can quickly change to a dark brown, and when this happens, the black spots become white. There is also another color phase in which the fish shows a banded pattern.

range and diet

The Graysby is a common fish where it is found: from Bermuda and the Bahamas and Florida to the hump of Brazil, including the Gulf of Mexico (Böhlke & Chaplin). This is a fearless little fish that will often eat from the diver's hand, even though smaller serranids are normally wary. The Graysby feeds primarily on small fishes and also eats shrimps, stomatopods, crabs, and gastropods (Randall). It stays near the bottom around and on coral reefs and rock formations where there is abundant shelter, and frequently it has been observed in caves. It is not normally a deep-water fish, but one individual was photographed at 240 feet off Texas.

family and growth cycle

The Graysby is born a female and changes into a male in the later stages of life. The pictured specimen has an obvious bulge abouts its middle section, an indication that it either is a pregnant female or a Graysby of indistinguishable gender that has just eaten.

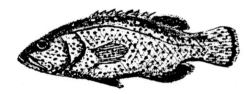

photo by Carl Roessler

Photo taken in 30 feet of water off Bonaire. Roessler used a Nikon F camera with a 55mm lens, a Bauer strobe, Kodachrome 25 film. Shot at 1/60 second at f/11, 15 inches from the subject.

Drawing: White-spotted phase

Harlequin Bass

(Serranus tigrinus)

physical characteristics

For most people the term "harlequin" brings to mind the pictures of Picasso's brightly decorated clowns, mute pantomimists wearing skin-tight, multicolored garbs. This must have been the vision of the ichthyologist who named the wildly patterned Harlequin Bass, a fish that has spots, stripes, and dashes. Because of its wild color pattern, the Harlequin Bass cannot be mistaken for any other bass in the west Atlantic. The dark markings are brown or black, with the light areas white or slightly yellow. Prominent spots near the front and back of the dorsal fin are also a noticeable characteristic of the fish. In spite of its bright appearance, the Harlequin Bass can effectively camouflage itself against the ocean bottom. The juvenile Harlequin Bass has more dark horizontal markings than do the adults. As the fish grows, the vertical bars become more prominent, and a vertical line or stripe forms to conceal the eye.

family and habits

The Harlequin Bass belongs to the genus *Serranus* within the family Serranidae of sea basses and groupers. As is characteristic of the small size of the species of *Serranus,* the Harlequin Bass only grows to about 4 inches. The small basses are not as easy going as their larger grouper relatives, and the Harlequin Bass will often dart away at the approach of a diver. Most of the larger serranids stay on or near the bottom, while the smaller individuals flit about near protective caves or holes in the reef. The Harlequin Bass stays near the bottom in grass beds or on coral and rock formations, and moves away at any sign of danger. It is found in depths between 8 and 80 feet and in habitats from the shoreline to 120 feet offshore.

range

The Harlequin Bass is found throughout the West Indies, from Bermuda, the Bahamas, and south Florida to Curaçao, and off Yucatan. The diver most likely will see the fish by itself as it roams about the bottom in search of food, which primarily consists of crustaceans (shrimps and crabs) and a small amount of fish.

growth cycle

Like other small serranids, the Harlequin Bass is believed to be hermaphroditic, possessing both eggs and sperm at the same time.

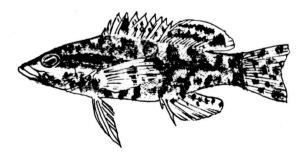

Photo by Carl Roessler

Photo taken in 35 feet of water off the island of Bonaire. Roessler used a Nikon F camera with a 55mm lens, a Bauer strobe, and Kodachrome II film. Shot at 1/60 second at f/11, 15 inches from the subject.

Creole Fish

(Paranthias furcifer)

general remarks

The deeply forked tail may be the most obvious characteristic of the Creole Fish. It was certainly observed by the ichthyologist who gave the fish its generic name, since *furcifer* comes from Latin words meaning "I bear a forked tail." *Paranthias* is composed of the Greek word for "near" and the ancient Latin name for fish, *anthias.* The Creole Fish has been thought to be similar or related to the ancient Anthias, and in body shape it resembles the Red Sea *Anthias* represented in this book. The Red Sea *Anthias* is a smaller fish (about half the size of the Creole Fish), but it has a similar forked tail.

physical characteristics

Overall, the Creole Fish is either a reddish brown or a dark gray, shading to a pale salmon in the region of the belly. There is a bright red-orange spot at the upper base of the pectoral fin. Although it is not obvious on the pictured specimen, there are usually three small white spots along the back, above the lateral line.

range, habits, and diet

Randall observed the Creole Fish primarily in littoral, inshore areas in the tropical Atlantic (Caribbean) and eastern Pacific. Ray and Ciampi reported it in areas from Cape San Lucas to the Galapagos Islands, Cuba to Brazil. It is a small fish and reaches ony 10 to 12 inches in length. It is relatively common where found, in depths ranging from 30 to 200 feet and always near reefs. The Creole Fish schools with others of the species, hovering above the reef in midwater to feed on planktonic animals which it picks out one by one from the passing water mass. At any sign of danger it darts for shelter in the typical style of the smaller serranids. This behavior is another similarity the Creole Fish shares with the Red Sea *Anthias,* which also schools in midwater. In studying the feeding habits of the Creole Fish, Randall notes that the small mouth, small teeth, numerous gill rakers, fusiform body, and deeply forked caudal fin are departures from the typical bass or grouper morphology, and that they are all specializations for midwater feeding on zooplankton. Specifically, the Creole Fish eats copepods (the largest part of its diet), tunicates, shrimps and shrimp larvae, amphipods, and fish larvae. This diet is an additional departure from a serranid trait; usually the sea basses are carnivorous and feed mostly on fishes and benthic crustaceans. Perhaps these differences are reasons why the Creole Fish is sometimes grouped separately in its own subfamily.

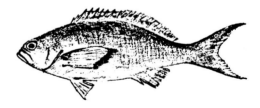

photo by Carl Roessler

The photo was taken in 40 feet of water off Bonaire. Roessler used a Nikon F camera with a 55mm lens, Bauer strobe, and Kodachrome 25 film. Shot at 1/60 second, at f/11, 14 inches from the subject.

Scalefin Anthias

(Anthias squamipinnis)

general remarks and range

The Scalefin Anthias is one of the most common schooling fishes of the Red Sea, with giant orange clouds of them swarming over isolated corals on shallow reefs. It is found from the coast of east Africa to the western Pacific. It is a brightly colored fish—the female orange and yellow, the males purplish red and finely spotted with yellow. The fish is small, growing to a maximum size of about 5 inches.

family

The genus *Anthias* is included in the subfamily Anthiinae of the family Serranidae. Like all serranids these fishes have large mouths, and their scales are ctenoid. They are sex changers, beginning as females and turning into males later in life. In behavior and in at least one physical characteristic (the deeply forked tail) the Scalefin Anthias resembles the Creole Fish of the Caribbean; the scientific name of the Creole Fish, *Paranthias* ("near anthias") *furcifer* seems to indicate an ichthyological connection, but in fact there is no relationship between the two. In addition to the forked tails, the cigar-shaped bodies are also very similar, although the Creole Fish is about twice the size of the Scalefin Anthias. The Scalefin Anthias has been called Goldfish in the past, but Randall points out that the generic name *Anthias* is catching on as a common name in the same manner that fishes in the *Chromis* genus are commonly called Chromis. "Scalefin" is in reference to the fin scales of *Anthias* and is the source of the *squamipinnis* name, which means "scaly fin."

growth cycle and physical characteristics

As is typical of the serranids, the Scalefin Anthias is born as a female, small and orange, and later in life grows into a male with a brighter color pattern of red and reddish purple marked with yellow and bright pink. The older male Scalefin Anthias has a more elongate third dorsal spine that trails out into a filament, and the upper and lower lobes of the caudal fin are filamentous. The tail of the younger fish is deeply forked or crescent-shaped, but without the filaments. The sex-reversal phenomenon of the Scalefin Anthias was studied in depth by the Israeli ichthyologists Dan Popper and Lev Fishelson, who determined that in a large group of *A. squamipinnis* containing hundreds of thousands of individuals, 80 to 90 percent of the fishes were sub-adult and adult females with only a few of them active territorial males. The scientists isolated a female-only group of 20 fishes, and within a week one of the females became male. The male was removed, and soon afterward another female became male. The procedure was repeated until at the end of a year all 20 fishes had become male. The scientists surmised that the transformation took place only if there was a reproductive need for males.

range and diet

The Scalefin Anthias is the most common of the shallow-water Indo-Pacific Anthiinae, and it is also the most well known of the species. It is a shy fish, usually staying within its protective school or in the cracks and ledges of a deep-water reef. It quickly swims for shelter when frightened. Its diet consists mainly of plank-tonic crustaceans—copepods, amphipods, shrimps—which it feeds on by day. The fish is highly prized among aquarists, but in captivity it can lose its bright color. It is said to keep its brightness if given heavy feedings of brine shrimp.

photo by Chris Newbert

Photo was taken in the Red Sea using a Canon F-1 with a 50mm macro lens in a Farallon/Oceanic Hydro 35, and a Farallon/Oceanic 2003 strobe, with Kodachrome 25 film. Shot at f/16, 10 inches from subject.

Barred Hamlet

(Hypoplectrus puella)

physical characteristics

The Barred Hamlet is said to be the most common of the hamlets, and while it may not be one of the most strikingly colored of its kind, it has characteristic markings that identify the species. The fish is yellowish overall, with four or five vertical dark-brown bars on the body. Almost center is the largest of the dark bars, which narrows toward the belly of the fish. The pale sections between the bars are accentuated with vertical blue lines. A bright blue line encircles the eye and continues down onto the cheek. Other iridescent blue spots, lines, and markings on the head, around the eye, and often on the soft dorsal distinguish the species from other hamlets. The blue eye stripes also appear in the Butter Hamlet *(H. unicolor),* but the latter fish has a black blotch at the base of its tail. The juvenile Barred Hamlet has two black spots at the tail, one on top of the other, and above each black spot is a squarish white blotch. The maximum size of the Barred Hamlet varies. Randall found that off west Florida these fish reach nearly 6 inches, but that in Antillean localities they reach not quite 5 inches.

habits and range

The Barred Hamlet is commonly seen on shallow reefs, usually a few feet off the bottom and always close to cover, a behavioral characteristic of the smaller members of the Serrranidae. The fish usually lives in depths of less than 75 feet. While many Caribbean fish are also found off South America and north along the U.S. coast, the hamlets are more or less confined to Bermuda, the Florida Keys, and the Gulf coast of Florida. They are common fishes and easy to approach.

diet

The Barred Hamlet, like all serranids, is carnivorous and eats shrimps (51 percent), crabs (21 percent), fishes (10 percent), and a small amount of mysids and stomatopods (Randall).

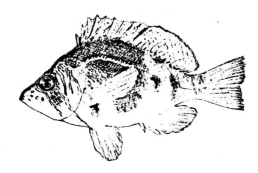

photo by Jack McKenney

Photo was taken in 6 feet of water off Anthony's Key, Roatan, Honduras. McKenney used a Nikon F camera, Oceanic housing, Honeywell strobe, and Kodachrome X film. Shot at 1/60 second at f/8, 18 inches from the subject.

Butter Hamlet

(Hypoplectrus unicolor)

physical characteristics

The Butter Hamlet is probably most distinguished by the big black spot at the base of its tail. While many hamlet species have significant black saddlelike spots in this area during juvenile stages, there is no other hamlet that maintains the spot during adulthood (except perhaps for a yet unidentified species of hamlet from Colombia, called the Blacktail Hamlet; this fish, however, has an entirely black tail). As long as hamlets are primarily identified by their color patterns and markings, the spot makes the identification of the Butter Hamlet relatively uncomplicated. The Butter Hamlet has been referred to simply as

"Hamlet" by some ichthyologists and is very similar to *Hypoplectrus puella* (the Barred Hamlet). However, the two are distinguished from each other by the black tail spot of *H. unicolor.* Both species have iridescent blue markings about the head, and the fin coloration of the two is similar, with the ventral fins rimmed in blue. The Butter Hamlet does not have bars, and overall is yellowish gray, becoming almost white ventrally. Very often there is a blue-edged black spot on the snout, but this is missing on our pictured specimen.

range

While the Barred Hamlet is the most common hamlet in the West Indies, the Butter Hamlet is reportedly rare in the West Indies but common in the Florida Keys. At one time all of the

hamlets were thought to be different color phases of one hamlet and were referred to as *H. unicolor,* which may be one reason why this species is often referred to as "Hamlet."

family and diet

Hamlets belong to the Serranidae and are small and compressed. Where most serranids stay near the substrate, the hamlets swim a few inches off the bottom in moderately deep water (40 to 70 feet). Normally they stay close to some sort of shelter. Their diet consists of small crustaceans such as shrimp and crabs, and they also eat small fishes, polychaetes, and stomatopods (Randall).

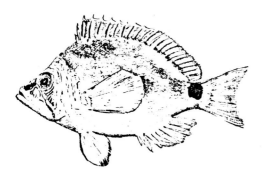

photo by Paul Tzimoulis

Photo was taken in 35 feet of water off Curacao. Tzimoulis used a Nikon F camera, 55mm Micro Nikkor lens in a Niko-Mar housing, 6B flash bulb, and Ektachrome X film. Shot at 1/125 second, f/22, 14 inches from subject.

Golden Hamlet

(Hypoplectrus gummigutta)

physical characteristics

Gummigutta means "gum-drop" and is a descriptive scientific name for the bright Golden Hamlet that lives on Caribbean reefs. The brilliant orange-yellow body is distinctive among the species of *Hypoplectrus* because it is bright and without vertical bars or smudges of darker colors. The blue-black splotch on the nose is another distinctive characteristic, one that is shared by the Shy Hamlet *(H. guttavarius).* However, the Shy Hamlet has a body that is dark purplish-brown for the most part, whereas the Golden Hamlet is a monotone gold, a coloration distinctive and beautiful.

range and habits

The Golden Hamlet is not as common as the other hamlets, and it occurs in deeper water, on the average, than the others. Böhlke and Chaplin observed only one individual of this species at a depth of 120 feet in the Exumas, Great Bahama Bank. Randall collected one specimen at a depth of 130 feet off the Dominican Republic. The range of the Golden Hamlet is limited. To date it is known only from the above locales, and also from Puerto Rico, Cuba, and Jamaica. Like most serranids, the Golden Hamlet stays near the bottom where it forages for crustaceans—largely shrimps, crabs, and fishes, with a small amount of mysids, stomatopods, and isopods (Randall).

family

The Golden Hamlet is a member of the Serranidae. It has the basslike body, although it is deeper, and in some respects similar to the damselfish shape. It has the large mouth of the serranid, ctenoid scales, and a continuous vertical line.

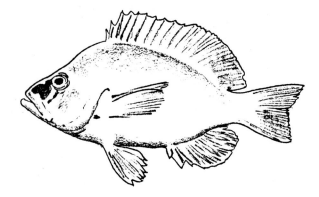

photo by Charles Arneson

Photo was taken in 60 feet of water off Salinas, Puerto Rico. Arneson used a Nikon F and a 105mm micro Nikkor lens in an Ikelite housing with a Honeywell 782 strobe and Kodachrome 25 film. Taken at f/16, 2 feet from the subject.

Soapfishes

(Family Grammistidae)

Greater Soapfish

(Rypticus saponaceus)

general remarks

If a soapfish is handled by humans or thrown into a bucket of water where it thrashes around, it will turn the water into a froth. The fish secretes a mucous over its body, and when disturbed, the slime turns to a soapy foam. The genetic name of the fish comes from this characteristic. The word *rypticus* is Greek for "washing," and *saponaceus* is Latin for "soapy." This slime is a natural defense against predators, since it has been found to contain a toxic protein. Ichthyologist John Randall discovered this after spearing a specimen and placing it inside his swim trunks; the slime was strongly irritating. Randall found no soapfishes in the stomachs of predatory fishes, and feeding experiments led him to conclude that the toxic slime of *Rypticus* is repelling to predators. The Greater Soapfish feeds on small fishes (mainly wrasses), as well as shrimps, crabs, and stomatopods.

photo by Peter Capen

Photo was taken in 30 feet of water off the island of Bonaire. Capen used a Rolleimarin with a No. 2 close-up lens, a Honeywell 810 strobe, and Ektachrome X film. Shot at 1/250 second, f/22, 16 inches from the subject.

family

Soapfishes are basslike fishes which grow to about 12 or 13 inches in length. Ichthyologists generally group them in their own family, Grammistidae, although some scientists still classify them as a subfamily of the Serranidae. In addition to the possession of the skin toxin grammistin, soapfishes are characterized by having the upper edge of the gill cover attached by skin to the body, small scales which are often embedded, and the fifth pelvic ray broadly attached by membrane to the abdomen (Randall).

physical characteristics

Rypticus saponaceus is the largest of all the soapfishes, and because of its size it is called the Greater Soapfish. It is also the most common soapfish in the Bahamas, closely followed in frequency by *R. subbifrenatus* (Spotted Soapfish). *R. saponaceus* is the only Bahaman soapfish with a color pattern of pale blotches on a darker background; all others have dark spots on a paler background (Böhlke & Chaplin). The juvenile *R. saponaceus*, however, has small dark spots on pale background and in this

stage could be confused with *R. bistrispinus* (Freckled Soapfish). The overall color of the adult *R. saponaceus* is usually brown, although it can be gray or nearly black, with irregular blotches of gray or pale brown on the sides. The juveniles, with their dark spots on a pale background, assume their adult coloration as the dark spots grow and merge to form the ground color, while the pale areas become blotches. Fish of about 2 inches in length have usually assumed the full adult color pattern (Böhlke & Chaplin).

range

The Greater Soapfish is found in shallow water areas on both sides of the Atlantic. In the western Atlantic it occurs off Bermuda, in the West Indies, and from Florida to Brazil, including the central American coast. In the eastern Atlantic it has been found off west Africa. Böhlke and Chaplin have recorded it in the Bahamas from the Little Bahama, Great Bahama, and Cal Say Banks, and from Hogsty Reef. The fish prefers a bottom of eroded limestone or mixed sand and rocks. Although often found in shallow water, it may occur in depths of 100 feet or more.

Basslets

(Family Grammatidae)

The family Grammatidae (a recent name change from Grammidae) comprises the tiny relatives of groupers and sea basses that are commonly known as basslets; members of the genus *Gramma* are often called grammas. The lateral line of the Serranidae is complete and continuous, while that of the grammatids is interrupted or absent. There are three species of *Gramma* in the tropical western Atlantic: *Gramma loreto, G. melacara,* and *G. linki.* The family appears to be restricted to the western Atlantic.

Fairy Basslet

(Gramma loreto)

physical characteristics

The Fairy Basslet, sometimes called Royal Gramma, is a small fish no more than 3 inches long. It is easily identified by the striking purple-and-yellow color pattern that makes the fish a favorite of aquarists. The front half of the body is vivid purple, the back portion is chrome yellow, and a prominent black spot accents the top of the forward part of the dorsal fin. There is a thin black line through the eye. The dividing area between the purple and yellow portions of the fish varies, depending upon where it lives. For example, the purple section is larger in individuals from the Virgin Islands and Haiti than in those from the Bahamas (Böhlke & Randall). The brightly colored pattern of the fish is very similar to the young Spanish Hogfish (*Bodianus rufus),* which is purple-blue about the head, yellow-orange at the posterior part, and which has the black spot in the dorsal area. However, the colors are different, with the young Spanish Hogfish more blue and pale yellow as compared to the purple and chrome yellow of the Fairy Basslet. The Fairy Basslet also swims in a short jerky fashion, as compared to the long gliding movements of the young hogfish. The head shapes of the two are different—round on the basslet, and pointed on the hogfish.

habits and diet

Basslets usually live in caves or beneath ledges, where they are often observed hanging upside down. They do this because they automatically orient themselves to the substrate. They are wary little fishes, darting into the darkest corners of the reef when frightened. Like the serranids, the basslets are carnivorous, feeding primarily on small planktonic crustaceans such as copepods, mysids, and shrimp larvae (Randall).

range and habitat

This fish is recorded from Bermuda and the Bahamas, through the Greater and Lesser Antilles, to the islands off Venezuela (Böhlke & Chaplin). It is not present off Florida, but in the Bahamas it is common everywhere. *Gramma loreto* is the "shallow-water" gramma, while *G. melacara* (Blackcap Basslet) occurs in deeper water, and *G. linki* occurs in still deeper water. *G. loreto* has been collected from the surface to depths of 200 feet, but it is more common in the shallower depths, whereas *G. melacara* is found in depths from 40 feet to 200 feet and is rare above 80 feet. Essentially, where one leaves off, the other is found.

photo by David Doubilet

Photo was taken in 185 feet of water on the Wall off Small Hope Bay, Andros Island. Doubilet used a Rolleimarin with a No. 5 bulb and Ektachrome X film. Shot at 1/125 second, f/11, 12 inches from the subject.

Bigeyes

(Family Priacanthidae)

Glasseye

(Priacanthus cruentatus)

general remarks

A loose generality could be made about red fishes with big eyes: For the most part they are nocturnally active, hiding under ledges by day and venturing out to feed at night. There are several families of these nighttime fishes: squirrelfishes (Holocentridae), sweepers (Pempheridae), cardinalfishes (Apogonidae), and bigeyes (Priacanthidae). The Glasseye is priacanthid, a fish family characterized by large eyes (thus the common name bigeye) and a predominantly red coloration. These fishes are also called *catalufas,* which comes from the Spanish word for a brightly colored material used to make carpets. The glasseye is sometimes called glasseye snapper, but it is not a snapper (family Lutjanidae).

range and habits

The Glasseye has a worldwide distribution. It is found in the west Atlantic, Caribbean, Pacific, and Indian Oceans,

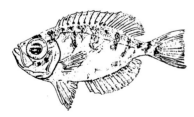

and is common around the Hawaiian Islands, where it is called *aweoweo* (redfish). In Hawaii big schools of these fishes have been known to appear near shore at night. Some of the early Hawaiians who were superstitious saw the "coming of the redfish" as doom for some members of the royal family. Ordinarily, the Glasseye was simply considered a good food fish, and the natives caught, dried, and ate it as a matter of course. In the West Indies the Glasseye is called *ojon,* or *ojudo* as well as *catalufa.* It is a shallow-water inhabitant, living in depths as little as 6 feet. Normally, the fish hides in protective holes, cracks, or crevices by day and ventures out over the reef at night to feed. However, the fish is not entirely nocturnal, as evidenced by the presence of fresh food in its stomach during daylight hours (Randall). The Glasseye is carnivorous and feeds primarily on fishes, polychaetes, crabs, and shrimps and their larvae, with most of the diet consisting of large planktonic animals.

physical characteristics

The Glasseye grows to about 1 foot in length. The young have a black margin around the caudal fin and are often seen in dense schools. The adults

are generally deep red with a silver mottling that can be highly variable. Usually there are narrow, vertical silver bars on the upper part of the body, and sometimes the silver coloration spreads all over, appearing as round spots on the lower half of the fish. Some individuals are almost entirely red, while others are largely silver. Some variations are attributed to environment, since the fish can exhibit more silver as it swims over a white sand bottom. The word *cruentatus* comes from the Latin for "bloody," in reference to the red color of the fish. The Glasseye closely resembles the Bigeye *(P. arenatus),* but it is distinguishable from the Bigeye because of its shorter pelvic fins. There is also a prominent flattened spine in *P. cruentatus* at the angle of the preopercle, which *P. arenatus* doesn't have. *P. arenatus* is also a deeper water species than *P. cruentatus.*

photo by Paul Humann

Photo was taken in 30 feet of water at Eden Rock, Grand Cayman Island. Humann used a Nikonos with a 28mm lens, Subsea 150 strobe, and ASA 64 film. Shot at f/18, 2½ feet from the subject.

Cardinalfishes

(Family Apogonidae)

Belted Cardinalfish

(Apogon townsendi)

family

Cardinalfishes (Apogonidae) are characterized by two well-developed dorsal fins, large eyes, and large mouths. Some, and possibly all, of the apogonid fishes are oral brooders, incubating eggs in the mouth. Most evidence points to the male as the incubator of eggs. There are 20 shallow-water species of cardinalfishes in the western Atlantic, but new species are being discovered all the time, principally in the Indo-Pacific.

general remarks

Hiding by day and very small in size, the Belted Cardinalfish is not among the most noticeable of Caribbean reef inhabitants. A sharp-eyed diver might see these tiny fishes by taking the time to look into the deep, dark holes in the reef, under ledges, or even inside shell cavities. At night they are in the open and easily approached. They and other cardinalfishes are nocturnal, leaving their hiding places to feed when the sun goes down. Like the squirrelfishes and bigeyes, red is the predominant color of the cardinalfishes (which is the basis for the family common name), and the eyes are large. In the Belted Cardinalfish the red is a translucent, coppery hue which can turn quite pale, depending upon the environment in which the fish is swimming. Through the translucence one can see the inside peritoneum through the body wall.

physical characteristics

The Belted Cardinalfish grows to only 2½ inches, and it is distinctive for its dark, broad "belt" at the base of the tail.

There is a thin bar just in front of this marking. (In our pictured specimen the belt is so light that the fish appears to have three thin vertical bars.) *A. binotatus,* the Barred Cardinalfish, is a similar-looking species with two well-separated, narrow, dark bars on the caudal peduncle, a longer snout, and smaller eyes.

habits, diet, and range

Where they occur, there are good-sized populations of cardinalfishes. These fishes live in depths from a few feet to several hundred feet. At night they have been observed several feet above the bottom where they appear to feed mainly on small crustaceans in the plankton (Randall). The Belted Cardinalfish has been recorded from the Bahamas and Florida to Curacao.

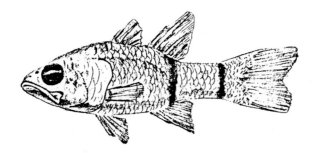

photo by Frank Trousdale

Photo was taken at night in 30 feet of water off Grand Cayman on the Balboa wreck. Trousdale used a Canon F1 in a Hydro 35 housing with a flat port, Subsea Mark 150 strobe. Shot at 1/60 second at f/16, 1 foot from the subject.

Jacks, Scads, and Pompanos

(Family Carangidae)

The jacks are swift, strong, silvery fishes that roam the open sea. Normally they will only swim into a reef area to feed on other smaller fishes, many of which become easy targets for the predator's unexpected, lightning-quick strikes. Jacks belong to the Carangidae, a diverse group which also includes scads and pompanos. The body shapes of the carangids vary greatly, including the elongated, cigar-shaped scads *(Decapterus)*, the deeper-bodied but swift-looking jacks *(Caranx)*, the even deeper-bodied and flattened pompanos *(Trachinotus)*, and the extremely thin and deeply profiled *Selene*.

While all of these fishes appear quite different, they have several common characteristics: slanting foreheads, deeply forked tails, and a pair of anal spines just in front of the anal fin. These spines can lie flat in a groove and so will not always be apparent. In the juveniles the spines are connected by a membrane and appear to be one continuous fin.

The Carangidae includes about 140 species around the world in both temperate and tropical waters (Smith-Vaniz). They are believed to spawn offshore, and the eggs drift with the plankton until they metamorphose into juveniles. Young carangids continue to drift in the protective shelter of sargassum weed, floating jellyfish, or even clumps of debris. As adults they do not inhabit reefs, but only approach them to feed on small fishes.

The pelagic open-ocean stage of juvenile carangids is one reason why some species have such a wide range.

African Pompano

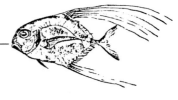

(Alectis ciliaris)

physical characteristics

The juvenile African Pompano looks as if it could only have been created by Mother Nature in one of her more whimsical moments. Called the Threadfish in its youth, the fish is easily singled out by long streamers which are actually extensions of the first rays of the dorsal and anal fins. *Ciliaris* (a recent name replacement for *crinitus*) means "hair," in reference to these streamers. The filamentous extensions are sometimes much longer than the entire fish, but as the Threadfish grows, the "threads" become shorter. However, adults up to 2 feet long have been reported with long filamentous fin rays that probably escaped normal wear and tear.

family

The African Pompano belongs to the Carangidae, along with the jacks and scads. Carangids are notably deeper-bodied as juveniles, becoming longer and slimmer as they grow. They typically have two detached spines just in front of the anal fin. However, in large adult African Pompanos these two anal-fin spines, along with the spinous dorsal fin, can become completely grown over.

habits and range

The adult African Pompano is a strong, fighting game fish usually found in open water often in depths over 100 feet. In contrast the juvenile African Pompano (Threadfish) stays inshore and lives near or under floating objects. The African Pompano is circumtropical in distribution (found in all tropical seas) and occurs on both sides of the Atlantic Ocean; in the west Atlantic it is found as far north as Massachusetts along the east coast of the United States, and south to Brazil, including the Gulf of Mexico (Böhlke & Chaplin). Ray found that the Threadfish is not timid and in contrast to most jacks can be approached quite closely.

photo by Carleton Ray
drawing: Adult

Snappers

(Family Lutjanidae)

Snappers are so called because they snap. They are popular food fishes, but because of this snapping behavior, fishermen catching them on a line must handle them with care. The snappers comprise a large family of fishes, the Lutjanidae, with approximately 250 species found all over the world. Many of them are highly prized in the commercial fishing industry.

Most snappers can be distinguished by their profiles. They have long, pointed faces, often referred to as the "snapper look." However, there are snappers that look like sea basses (Serranidae). Snappers have smaller mouths than basses, and the maxilla is not fully exposed on the cheek; many of them have yellowish fins. Within the snapper family some species are separated by complicated technical determinations such as tooth patterns, but quite often the color patterns alone are adequate for identification.

Many snappers are shallow-water inshore fishes living near the bottom, where they can easily find a hole in which to hide. Others, such as the commercially exploited Red Snapper *(Lutjanus purpureus)*, are deep-water dwellers. The Yellowtail Snapper *(Ocyurus chrysurus)* is a mid-water fish, often cruising well above reefs. The juvenile snappers of some species enter mangroves and estuaries where fresh water and salt water mix, and in these nursery grounds they grow up with a wide variety of other marine fishes. Snappers have enlarged canine teeth and are carnivorous. They feed primarily at night on fishes and crustaceans such as shrimps and crabs.

Most snappers are not easily approached by the diver, and in keeping with their nocturnal habits they hide in huddled masses by day and come out to feed at night. The juveniles, however, are easily approached in their estuarine nursery grounds.

Schoolmaster

(Lutjanus apodus)

general remarks

The Schoolmaster is the most common of the Caribbean snappers (Lutjanidae), and has been recorded from a variety of habitats ranging from coral reefs to tidepools. Randall reports that he most often has seen the Schoolmaster among stands of elkhorn coral, while Böhlke and Chaplin report most of their specimens inhabiting tidal creeks lined with mangroves. This snapper seems to live in every type of environment within its range.

physical characteristics

The fins of the Schoolmaster are all yellowish, and this is the chief distinguishing characteristic of the fish.

habits and diet

Most snappers are not easily approached by the diver. The Schoolmaster is shy by day, spreading out from its protective huddle only at night to feed over the reefs. The Schoolmaster apparently is more confined to reefs than other snappers (Randall) and feeds primarily on fishes (60 percent) and crabs (22 percent), the rest of the diet being composed of stomatopods, shrimps, octopuses, gastropods, and unidentified crustaceans. The larger individuals feed more on fishes, while the smaller ones feed more on crustaceans.

range

The Schoolmaster is found on both sides of the Atlantic; in the west Atlantic it has been recorded from Massachusetts (where there are a few young stragglers) and Bermuda to Brazil, including the Gulf of Mexico. The Schoolmaster is very common in the Bahamas, where, true to its name, it schools during the day under ledges or inside holes in the reef.

photo by George Marler

Photo taken in 30 feet of water on the wreck of the Rhone, British Virgin Islands. Marler used a Nikonos with a Seacor 21mm lens, Subsea Mark 150 strobe, and Kodachrome 64 film. Shot at f/11, 3 feet from the subject.

Yellowtail Snapper

(Ocyurus chrysurus)

characteristics

Ocyurus comes from two Greek words meaning "swift tail," and *chrysurus* means "golden tail"; together the words provide the species name for the Yellowtail Snapper. Known simply to many divers as the Yellowtail, the fish is one of the most common of the west Atlantic reefs. The coloration and markings of the Yellowtail Snapper set it apart from any other snapper of its range. As its name implies, it has a very large, deeply forked, yellow tail. An easily recognizable lateral, yellow stripe extends along the mid-body region from the snout to the tail, broadening as it reaches the tail. Above this stripe are blotches of yellow over a basic ground color of light blue. Below the line are thin, pale-yellow stripes. The coloration of the fish varies with individual specimens: some have a reddish cast bordering the underside of the yellow stripe, and the ground color above the stripe can vary between light silver-blue to olive or even violet. However, all of the fins of the Yellowtail Snapper are yellow, and the bright yellow stripe along the mid-body is unchanged and unmistakable.

family, habits, and diet

The Yellowtail Snapper is a member of the Lutjanidae, and it is unique in the family because it frequently cruises in open water between the surface and the top of the reef. Snappers normally stay close to the bottom or in their protective holes, but the Yellowtail Snapper will often be seen out during the day. It is swift-swimming and, where spear-fishing occurs, it is among the wariest of fishes. In marine preserves where divers feed fishes, it readily takes food at close quarters, which may indicate a high intelligence among fishes (Randall). All snappers have enlarged canine teeth and are carnivorous. The Yellowtail Snapper feeds on fishes (small herring), crustaceans (shrimps and crabs), stomatopods, and annelid worms. Most snappers are strictly nocturnal feeders, but the Yellowtail Snapper does not restrict itself to feeding at night. Since it is a midwater feeder, its carnivorous diet includes a significant amount of planktonic or floating organisms such as salps, ctenophores, and pteropods. The juvenile Yellowtail Snapper is often encountered in turtle-grass beds and in mangrove areas; as they grow older, they head farther offshore. The fish reaches a length of 28 inches and a weight of 5 pounds.

range

The Yellowtail Snapper occurs on both sides of the Atlantic; in the west Atlantic it is found from Massachusetts and Bermuda to south Florida and Brazil, including the Gulf of Mexico. It has been recorded in the Cape Verde Islands and is extremely popular in Cuba, where it is known as *rabirubia*. The Yellowtail Snapper is abundant in the West Indies and in the Bahamas, where it swims over a wide variety of underwater terrain: mud and sand bottoms, grass beds, coral reefs, and gorgonian beds.

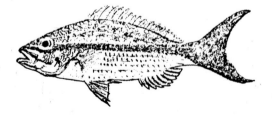

photo by Jack McKenney

Photo was taken in 50 feet of water on the Deep Reef off Freeport, Grand Bahama Island. McKenney used a Rolleimarin, Subsea strobe, and Ektachrome X film. Shot at 1/250 second at f/11, 3 feet from the subject.

Grunts

(Family Haemulidae)

Grunts do exactly what their name implies: they grunt. Their distinctive trademark is their ability to produce short, deep, gutteral sounds that are audible both underwater and topside. They accomplish this by grinding their pharyngeal teeth together, the sound amplified by the swim bladder. The Spanish name for the grunt is Ronco, which comes from "roncar" (to snore).

Haemulidae (now the accepted name for the family, replacing the name Pomadasyidae) comes from the Greek, meaning "bloody gums." This is in reference to the characteristic bright-red mouths of the grunts. Some of the grunts are known to engage in a "kissing" act in which two individuals come face to face with open mouths and push against each other. It is uncertain whether this behavior is a courtship ritual or an act of territorial aggression, but in either case, the subaqueous smooching of the grunts has long been a popular subject for underwater photographers.

The Haemulidae is very closely allied to the snappers (Lutjanidae), and ichthyologists separate the two families on the basis of their tooth structures. The snappers have stronger canine teeth, and grunts have pharyngeal teeth (located in the region of the pharynx, where the gills are lodged). By day the grunts congregate in schools, sometimes with upwards of 1,000 individuals in one group, and they all hang motionless in suspended animation.

Typical color patterns for haemulids often involve horizontal stripes, with blue and yellow being common colors. The juveniles characteristically have a black, lateral stripe which ends in a spot at the base of the tail. Both of these markings disappear with age in most species.

There are about 175 species of grunts in various oceans of the world, largely in tropical waters with a few forms extending into temperate waters.

White Grunt

(Haemulon plumieri)

physical characteristics

The White Grunt closely resembles the French Grunt (H. flavolineatum), but it is distinguished from the French Grunt by having larger scales above the lateral line than below it. The color pattern of the White Grunt varies, but the stripes on the head are always present.

photo by Jack McKenney

Photo was taken in 60 feet of water on the Deep Reef off Freeport, Grand Bahama. McKenney used a Rolleimarin, a Subsea strobe, and Ektachrome X film. Shot at 1/125 second, f/8, 24 inches from subject.

growth cycle

The juvenile White Grunt is distinctive from other young grunts in that it lacks the black stripe that is typically found in the juveniles. Immature haemulids are principally black and white with a black, lateral stripe and spot on the tail, but in the White Grunt the black markings are limited to the tail spot and the head, which is heavily spotted with black melanophores. As the fish grows, the black and white pattern is replaced by the blue and yellow coloration.

diet and habits

The adult *H. plumieri* feeds primarily on crabs (26 per-

cent), polychaetes (14.5 percent), and echinoids (12.4 percent), followed by sipunculids, gastropods, shrimps, fishes, and pelecypods.

range

The White Grunt is common and occurs on the east coast of the United States (from Cape Hatteras and Chesapeake Bay to Florida). It is found in large numbers on West Indies reefs and on sandy patches through the Gulf of Mexico and the Central American coast (Böhlke & Chaplin), usually in shallow water of around 20 feet.

Bluestriped Grunt

(Haemulon sciurus)

physical characteristics

This is one of the grunt species having a blue and yellow striped pattern (the other principal ones being *H. flavolineatum* and *H. sciurus*). The Bluestriped Grunt is distinctive in that it has horizontal stripes along the entire body, rather than horizontal stripes above the lateral line and diagonal below *(H. flavolineatum)* or on the head only *(H. plumieri)*. The scales are equal in size over the entire body, as compared to the other two species which have different-sized scales above and below their lateral lines. The most distinctive feature, however, is the blackish tail of the Bluestriped Grunt. (The tails of the other species are blue or yellow.) Several grunts have blackish tails, but they do not have yellow and blue striped patterns. The dorsal fin of the Bluestriped Grunt is also rimmed with black.

growth cycle and diet

The juvenile Bluestriped Grunt is similar to the young of other haemulids—small and fusiform with a blackish horizontal stripe down the middle of the body and a blotch near the tail. As it grows, it loses these markings and becomes blue and yellow. The fish is said to grow to 18 inches, making it one of the larger grunts, but it is more likely to reach about 13 to 15 inches. Like all grunts, this species is nocturnal, schooling around corals by day and spreading out to feed at night. The Bluestriped Grunt feeds mainly on crustaceans, mollusks, annelids, and some small ophiuroids (Randall).

range

The Bluestriped Grunt is very common in the West Indies and is most often encountered with *H. plumieri,* the White Grunt. The fish has been recorded in the waters of Bermuda and the Bahamas, and from South Carolina to southeastern Brazil, including the Gulf of Mexico and the Central American coast (Böhlke & Chaplin).

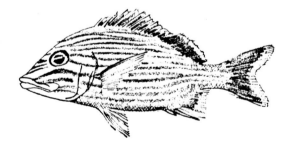

photo by Peter Capen

Photo taken in 35 feet of water in Georgetown Harbor off Grand Cayman Island. Capen used a Rolleimarin with a No. 2 close-up lens, Honeywell 810 strobe, and Ektachrome X film. Shot at 1/125 second at f/22, 18 inches from subject.

Porkfish

(Anisotremus virginicus)

general remarks

The Porkfish is a species of grunt (Haemulidae) of the genus *Anisotremus*. This genus is more porgylike and deeper bodied than the other grunts. The characteristic steep profile of the head forms an angle of about 45 degrees with one of the black bars on the side of the body.

physical characteristics

The two vertical black bars on the head and forebody are identifying physical features of the adult Porkfish. The frontal diagonal black band extends from the cavern of the mouth through the eye to the top of the head, while the bar in back of it crosses under the gills and extends to the top of the head. In back of these bands are alternating bars of silver-blue and yellow. All of the fins are yellow, as is the top of the head. The other species of *Anisotremus* in the western Atlantic, *A. surinamensis* (Black Margate), lacks the brilliant yellow coloring of the Porkfish and is more silver-gray. The Black Margate sometimes has the black bar through the eye, but when this appears, it is about four times as wide as the diameter of the eye, while the bar of the Porkfish is about the same width as the diameter of the eye.

growth cycle

The young Porkfish and the adult are entirely different in appearance. The body of the young Porkfish is a yellowish-white fading to a gray on the underside, with two black stripes that run horizontally along the sides. The lower stripe extends from the tail to the eye. There is a large spot at the base of the tail. While the juvenile has the yellow head and fins similar to those of the adult Porkfish, it completely lacks the two broad, vertical bands. The juvenile Porkfish is nearly identical in appearance to the juvenile Black Margate, but in the Porkfish the tail spot is large and distinct, whereas in the Black Margate the spot is smaller and less distinct. The Porkfish grows to about 12 inches in length. Young Porkfish have been known to act as cleaner fish, picking off parasites from larger fishes such as barracudas, snappers, or jacks.

diet

Because the juvenile Porkfish acts as a cleaner fish, it is assumed that ectoparasites form a significant part of its diet (Randall). The adults feed on ophiuroids, crabs, shrimps, and polychaetes, as well as a large number of other benthic invertebrates. All of the animals upon which the Porkfish preys are notably small (Randall). Like all grunts, the Porkfish is a nocturnal feeder, and they band together in schools for protection during the day, spreading out over flat, sandy bottoms at night to search for food.

range

The Porkfish is not common in Puerto Rico or the Virgin Islands, but it is abundant on coral reefs in the Florida Keys (Randall). It is known from Bermuda, the Bahamas, and Florida south to Brazil, including the Central American coast (Böhlke & Chaplin). Typically it stays in relatively shallow, inshore waters or near the protective shelter of the reef during daytime hours.

photo by Jack McKenney

Photo was taken in 55 feet of water off Freeport, Grand Bahama. McKenney used a Rolleimarin, Subsea strobe, No. 2 close-up lens, and Ektachrome X film. Shot at 1/250 second, f/8, 18 inches from the subject.

drawing: Juvenile

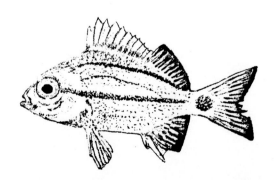

Croakers and Drums

(Family Sciaenidae)

The Sciaenidae are widely distributed throughout the oceans of the world, with about 160 species ranging in size from a few inches to 225 pounds. The species of *Equetus* within the family, which include the Jackknife Fish and the Spotted Drum in the Caribbean, are distinctive for their high dorsal fins and dark striped patterns. The drum and croaker names come from the fact that the fishes make audible drumming or croaking noises; the muscles attached to the swim bladder vibrate, and the bladder acts as a sound box to magnify the sound. Sciaenids without swim bladders are known to create noise by grinding their teeth together, which is an indication that the noisemaking has an important function. Ichthyologists have noted that the sound activity of the fishes increases during the spawning season, and that noise patterns vary between night and day.

The juveniles of both the croakers and drums are very similar in that they are white with black stripes and have high, trailing dorsal fins. In extremely young juveniles of both species the dorsal fin is often longer than the body of the fish. When the juveniles reach about 3 inches in length, the dorsal fin and the body begin to even out, the fin becoming comparatively shorter as the fish grows.

Sciaenids are known to use brackish coastal estuaries as nursery grounds for their young, and because of this many adult drums and croakers are found in coastal reef habitats. They are carnivores, and many of the sciaenids are known to be excellent food fishes.

Spotted Drum

(Equetus punctatus)

physical characteristics

The Spotted Drum has the characteristic "high hat" which resembles that of the related Jackknife Fish. This is the ribbonlike anterior dorsal which is often longer than the entire fish during the juvenile stage. As the fish grows (maximum size around 10 inches) the long dorsal becomes proportionately shorter in size. Other things also begin to happen with growth: the tail and second dorsal fins become black with white dots, and this is the source of the species name *punctatus,* which means "spotted" in Latin. The pectoral and anal fins are black, with the anal fin sometimes also acquiring white spots. The Spotted Drum gains more than one horizontal body stripe— usually one large midlateral stripe with two smaller stripes above and below it.

habits, range, and diet

This black and white fish with dots and stripes is a striking and beautiful sight on Caribbean reefs. It is solitary, rarely seen with others of its own kind. During the day it stays close to the reefs nearly always in shallow water. It is said to be somewhat secretive by nature, and ichthyologists have expressed their difficulties in collecting this particular species. Böhlke and Chaplin state that the Spotted Drum is the rarest species of its genus in the Bahamas. The Spotted Drum has been recorded from Florida through the West Indies. In the Bahamas it occurs off Nassau on the Great Bahama Bank (Böhlke & Chaplin). Sciaenids are carnivores, and Spotted Drums feed mainly on crabs, shrimps, and polychaetes (Randall). Many of the sciaenids are excellent food fishes, but the small sizes of the *Equetus* species make these particular fishes better admired as natural works of art.

photo by Jack McKenney

Photo was taken in 30 feet of water at the Invisibles off Virgin Gorda, British Virgin Islands. McKenney used a Rolleimarin, Subsea strobe, and Ektachrome X film. Shot at 1/125 second at f/11, 1½ feet from the subject.

drawing: Juvenile

Jackknife Fish

(Equetus lanceolatus)

physical characteristics

With a high dorsal fin that looks like a blade and a body resembling the handle of a pocketknife, the Jackknife Fish is well named. The long dorsal fin of the juveniles can be higher than the fish is long, and because of this the fish is sometimes called "Ribbonfish" or "High Hat." *Lanceolatus* means "Lance-shaped," in reference to the physical characteristics of the dorsal fin. The adult Jackknife Fish *(Equetus lanceolatus)* and the adult Spotted Drum *(E. punctatus)* have similar colorations— black bands on a silver-white background, with one band passing through the eye. The Spotted Drum, however, develops white spots on the darkened dorsal, caudal, and anal fins, whereas in the Jackknife Fish these fins are pale. The black bands in the Jackknife Fish are limited to three: one passes through the eye, another extends from the top of the head to the ventral fin, and the last runs from the base of the dorsal fin through the tail. Although the juveniles of both species are very similar, the most noticeable difference between the two species is in the snouts: the young Jackknife Fish has a black line down the center of the snout, whereas the young Spotted Drum has a round black spot at the very tip.

range, habits, and diet

The Jackknife Fish is a west Atlantic fish, and has been recorded from the coasts of North and South Carolina, through the Bahamas and Bermuda, south to the hump of Brazil, including the Gulf of Mexico. The Jackknife Fish is common on offshore island reefs. This fish is a nocturnal feeder, and by day the diver may only see a few stragglers, each one usually alone on rock or coral reefs in depths around 40 feet. It is a carnivore, and when it ventures out from its protective hole or crevice at night, it forages for shrimps, polychaete worms, and crabs.

photo by George Marler

Marler took the photo in 40 feet of water off Salt Island in the British Virgin Islands. He used a Nikonos with a Seacor 21mm lens, Subsea Mark 150 strobe. Shot at f/16, 1/60 second, 18 inches from subject.

drawing: Juvenile

Goatfishes

(Family Mullidae)

Yellow Goatfish

(Mulloides martinicus)

family

Mulloides is a recent change from *Mulloidichthys,* which was an invalid generii. Goatfishes are sometimes called surmuletts. They are highly prized food fishes around the world. Böhlke and Chaplin describe the ancient Romans paying high prices in silver for the fish, which they often kept in elaborate saltwater ponds and attended better than sick servants. Today the goatfish is still considered a table delicacy.

general remarks and diet

Goatfishes have chin whiskers in the form of a pair of long barbels equipped with chemosensory organs which are used to hunt for food. As the goatfishes move along sand or mud flats, they feel and taste

photo by Carl Roessler

Photo was taken in 40 feet of water off Klein, Bonaire. Roessler used a Nikon F camera with a 55mm lens, a Bauer strobe, and Kodachrome 25 film. Shot at 1/60 second, f/11, 15 inches from the subject.

their way with the barbels, thrusting them into the bottom to find their prey. The prey usually consists of benthic invertebrates such as polychaetes, crabs, shrimps and their larvae, pelecypods, isopods, and chitons (Randall). Often the fishes will dig in with their entire snout to feed on these animals.

physical characteristics and habits

Very often the chin barbels are not obvious on goatfishes since they fold them back against the lower jaw when swimming. Aside from the barbels on the chin, the goatfishes are recognizable by their two widely separated dorsal fins and the forked tail. There are two species of goatfishes in the Caribbean, and they have widely different habits. The Yellow Goatfish more often is seen in large schools as it swims over the reefs, and by day it feeds very little. The Spotted Goatfish, *Pseudupeneus maculatus,* is more solitary and feeds during the day, grubbing its way along the bottom with its barbels. The Yellow Goatfish is distinctive because of the yellow fins and the yellow stripe that extends from the eye to the tail in much the same man-

ner as the Yellowtail Snapper *(Ocyurus chrysurus).* The Spotted Goatfish, on the other hand, has three blotches along the side of the body.

growth cycle and range

Postlarval goatfishes are pelagic, more silvery than the adults, and have dark-blue markings. As they grow, they settle down from the open-ocean currents to become bottom dwellers. The maximum size of the Yellow Goatfish is about 1 foot; Böhlke and Chaplin have noted that no juvenile Yellow Goatfish less than 4 inches long has been recorded. The fish is found throughout the West Indies and Bermuda, and from Florida to Brazil, including the Gulf of Mexico. The generic name *martinicus* means "from Martinique."

Spadefishes

(Family Ephippidae)

Long-Finned Spadefish

(Platax teira)

general remarks

Of all the spadefishes, *Platax teira,* or the Long-finned Spadefish, has the most extremely extended fins, with this characteristic being most pronounced in the juvenile stage. As the fish grows, these fins become proportionately shorter. The extended fins are the dorsal, anal, and pelvic fins, and it is the elongated pelvic fin that distinguishes the Long-finned Spadefish from other spadefishes.

growth cycle

The profile of the Long-finned Spadefish is higher than it is long, and during the juvenile stage the height of the fish can be several times its length. A 2-inch spadefish has been known to measure 6 inches in height. The adult fish reaches a total length of about 16 inches, although individuals reportedly have reached 2 feet and a weight of several pounds.

photo by Carl Roessler
Photo taken in 35 feet of water at Bartholomew Bay, Galapagos. Roessler used a Nikon F camera with a 55mm lens, a Bauer strobe, and Kodachrome II film. Shot at 1/60 second at f/16, 12 inches from the subject.

habits and diet

According to Dr. Gerald R. Allen of the Western Australian Museum, the Long-finned Spadefish is most often found on shallow coral reefs, in mangrove swamps, or in harbors around wharves and wreckage. The fish often lives in polluted areas, and it eats a wide variety of foods, including garbage or offal. For this reason, aquarists find the Long-finned Spadefish easy to keep, and it actually is considered a good "pet" that will eat from its master's hand at feeding time. This spadefish grows quickly (about 1 inch per month) and is fairly timid. Aquarists are cautioned about putting the fish with aggressive tank mates that could quickly make the long fins of the spadefish ragged.

family

The Long-Finned Spadefish is a member of the Ephippidae and displays interesting behavioral characteristics that are typical of the family. Spadefishes are great mimics in the juvenile phase, and during this time they will often disguise themselves by playing dead among dead leaves. It is difficult to tell the difference between leaf and fish, and this camouflage is a good defense against predators. This behavior is reminiscent of the juvenile Spadefish of the Atlantic *(Chaetodipterus faber),* which floats like debris in the currents.

physical characteristics

The spadefishes are compressed, deep-bodied fishes that resemble the butterflyfishes in some respects. All spadefishes of the genus *Platax* have a dark band through the eye and another through the pectoral fin base. The Long-finned Spadefish has other vertical bands which fade or disappear, depending upon the environment and whether or not the fish is alarmed. As the fish grows, the vertical bands become wider and more pronounced.

range

The Long-finned Spadefish is found throughout the tropical Indo-Pacific, off northern Australia, Indonesia, New Guinea, the Philippines, Okinawa, China, Japan, Ryukyu Islands, East Africa, Madagascar, Mauritius, Seychelles, and the Red Sea. In some of these localities, particularly in some areas of southeast Asia, the natives consider the Long-finned Spadefish a good food fish.

Left-eye Flounders

(Family Bothidae)

Peacock Flounder

(Bothus lunatus)

families

Flatfishes include the flounders, halibuts, sanddabs, soles, tonguefishes, and broadsoles. The Bothidae are the left-eyed flounders, in which the eyes are on the left side of the head. The Peacock Flounder is a left-eyed flounder (Bothidae). Left-eyed flounders will sometimes appear with their eyes on the right side of the head (and conversely, right-eyed flounders will appear with eyes on the left), but the distinction can still be made internally.

general remarks

The left-eyed flounders are an odd group of bottom-dwelling flatfishes that may bury themselves in the sand up to the eyes, which are positioned on one side of the head. There are many species of flatfishes in the world's oceans, and all of them lie on the bottom, sometimes burying their pancake-thin bodies for protection. During the larval stage one eye migrates over the top of the head so that both eyes are on one side when the fishes are ready to settle out of the pelagic, drifting state and transform into juveniles (Randall). This strange phenomenon is common to all species of flatfishes.

physical characteristics

The Peacock Flounder is the largest of the genus *Bothus* in the western Atlantic, growing to 18 inches. It is the most colorful of the left-eyed flounders, having many blue circles and spots spread over the top side of the gray/brown body. There are three distinct dark blotches along the midline of the body, the first and largest one being just behind the pectoral fin. Flounders are difficult to see, since they camouflage themselves nearly completely by changing colors to match their surroundings or by burying themselves in the sand. Sometimes the only time a diver will see this fish is if it is startled out of its hiding place.

range

The Peacock Flounder has been recorded from Bermuda, the Bahamas and Florida, south to Brazil, including the Central American coast (Böhlke & Chaplin). Its chosen habitat is sand—with either rock, turtle grass, or reef intermixed—in both deep and shallow water (10 feet being common). This flounder is also found in mangrove areas.

growth cycle

There are subtle differences between male and female flounders, the principal difference being that the eyes of the adult males are farther apart than those of the females. Larval flounders are nothing like the adults. In fact, the young ones start out like any ordinary fish, swimming vertically and freely, with eyes symmetrically located on both sides of the head. The young fishes then begin to lean to the right or left, gradually adapting themselves to the bottom. The eye on the underside begins to migrate, and the bones and mouth twist and contort all in the direction of topside. The pigment then disappears from the underside. The lovely blue-spotted decor of the Peacock Flounder is only on the left side of the fish; underneath the body is white.

photo by George and Luana Marler

Photo was taken in 20 feet of water off Norman Island, British Virgin Islands. The Marlers used a Nikon F with a 55mm lens in a Giddings/Felgen housing and a Subsea strobe. Shot at f/11, 18 inches from the subject.

Jawfishes

(Family Opistognathidae)

Yellowhead Jawfish

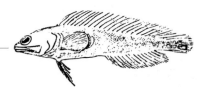

(Opistognathus aurifrons)

general remarks

Master engineer, diligent laborer, and general busybody—that's the jawfish. Whereas most fishes seem to live a relaxed existence, the jawfish keeps a full work schedule, excavating and building the tunnels in which it lives. This includes cleaning house, hauling rocks and sand with which to make repairs, and protecting the lair from would-be intruders. Because of its busy behavior, the jawfish is an extremely interesting and popular aquarium fish. Given enough sand and pebbles with which to build, the fish will carry on in the tank as it does in the sea.

family and physical characteristics

The jawfish family Opistognathidae is distinguished by a number of physical characteristics: large heads, big mouths, and long, tapering bodies. The fins (dorsal, anal, caudal, and ventral) are long, giving the fish an eellike appearance. The huge eyes are capable of rotating in any direction, but can be kept in horizontal focus. Most jawfishes are dark and dull, brown or black being the principal

colors. The Yellowhead Jawfish *(O. aurifrons)* of the Caribbean stands out with its golden head and pale blue-gray body. Sometimes pale blue dots are obvious on the blue section of the fish, and occasionally there are black spots on the chin. The Yellowhead Jawfish most closely resembles the Yellow Jawfish *(O. gilberti)*, except that *gilberti* is entirely yellow with no blue at all. In juvenile *aurifrons* (about 1 inch in length) the yellow on the head is limited to a small area, and the blue color is not evident on the body and fins. The Yellowhead Jawfish grows to 3½ to 4 inches in length.

habits, diet, and range

Some jawfishes are mouth-brooders, and the Yellowhead Jawfish is one of these. The male incubates the eggs in his mouth, spitting them into the burrow only to take time out to eat. The Yellowhead Jawfish feeds by hovering 6 to 8 inches above its lair (it is often seen in this position) and catching zooplankton from passing water currents. The fish is carnivorous, and aquarium specimens do well on brine shrimp. The hovering above the hole is a behavioral characteristic peculiar to the *O. aurifrons* species. Other jawfish

usually stay in their holes and stick their heads out to catch their drifting food (Böhlke & Chaplin). The diver most likely will see the Yellowhead Jawfish in shallow water, although it occurs in depths from 8 to 115 feet. In the Florida Keys it has been found at 135 feet. While other jawfish species are known to build their tunnels in the limestone substrate and colonize with different species, the Yellowhead Jawfish will build only around those of its own kind. A jawfish burrow can measure over a foot in length and is built by the fish scooping up sand and coral bits in its mouth. The fish then reinforces the sides of the tunnel with bits of rock to keep it from caving in. The Yellowhead Jawfish has been recorded from the Bahamas (Little Bahama, Great Bahama and Cay Sal Banks, and on Hogsty Reef), to Florida, Cuba, and the Virgin Islands.

photo by Bob Cunningham

Photo was taken in 25 feet of water off the Florida Keys. Cunningham used a Nikon F camera with an 85mm lens, "M" ring, EX film, and 6B flash bulb. Shot at 1/250 second, f/22, 18 inches from the subject.

Flying Gurnards

(Family Dactylopteridae)

Flying Gurnard

(Dactyloptena orientalis)

general remarks

The Flying Gurnard is a walking, armored birdfish of the ocean floor. Although there are reports that it can "fly" as do flying fishes, its heavily armored, boxlike body gives ichthyologists reason to believe that the fish doesn't fly at all. It is seen on the ocean bottom, where it walks around on strongly developed pectoral fins. The square, bony head is encased in an armor somewhat like a scorpionfish, and there is a single, long dorsal ray that can project straight up from the back of the head. The scales are tough and ridged, somewhat like the sharp, bony scutes of the jacks.

habits and diet

Very often divers will see the Flying Gurnard creeping around on the bottom in shallow, sandy areas 20 to 30 feet deep, where it feeds on benthic crustaceans, clams, crabs, and an occasional small

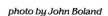

photo by John Boland

Photo was taken in 40 feet of water off Maui, Hawaii. Boland used a Rollei SL66 camera with 120mm lens, Hydro strobe, and Professional Ektachrome film. Shot at 1/30 second, f/11, 3½ feet from the subject.

fish. Randali has observed gurnards scratching in the sand with their short anterior pectoral rays as if searching for food. The big winglike pectorals are spread laterally when the fish is alarmed. However, the fish usually remains settled, its brown spots and blotches camouflaging it well against the general confusion of an ocean bottom. The fish has a relatively flat profile, which also contributes to its ability to remain lost to sight. The juveniles are similar to the adults, except that their pectoral wings are shorter. The adults grow to about 14 inches in length.

family

The Flying Gurnard belongs to the family Dactylopteridae. *Dactyloptena* comes from the Greek, meaning "finger" and "fern," which refers to the specialized fins that enable the fish to scratch for food and creep around. The dactylopterids might be confused with the sea robins (Triglidae), which also have large, brightly colored pectoral wings and the ability to walk on the bottom. The difference between the two families is in the arrangement of the head bones. In general, sea robins are bony all over, whereas the gurnards

have two separate dorsal fins and the single flagpolelike spine. Some ichthyologists have classified juvenile Flying Gurnards as *Cephalacanthus* and the adults as *Dactyloptena* (Jordan & Evermann).

range

Dactyloptena orientalis is found in the Indo-Pacific region. In the Hawaiian Islands it is called Lolo-oau, and in Australia, Purple Flying Gurnard. Other localities include New Guinea, Mauritius and the Cape of Good Hope, the East Indies, China, Japan, and into Melanesia and Polynesia. The Hawaiian Islands constitute the most northern reach of its range. A related species, *Dactyloptena volitans*, occurs in the Caribbean.

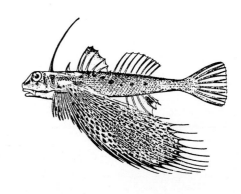

Angelfishes & Butterflyfishes

(Family Pomacanthidae)

(Family Chaetodontidae)

The angelfishes and butterflyfishes are the most beautiful fishes of any tropical reef. Their bright colors, expressed in imaginative patterns over their flat, pancake-thin bodies, are whimsical works of art—a joyful splash from Nature's great paintbrush. It is hard to imagine a tropical reef community without them, for they are spectacular highlights to the underwater seascape. In undersea parks where divers feed fishes, they are among the most inquisitive and will be the first to accept handouts, swimming up boldly to take bits of sea urchin or fish. All of them are the underwater photographer's dream

Here we treat angelfishes and butterflyfishes as separate families with a common introduction. For years ichthyologists placed them together in one family, Chaetodontidae, dividing them into the subfamilies Pomacanthinae (angelfishes) and Chaetodontinae (butterflyfishes).

The major feature the two families share is their tooth structure. *Chaetodont* means "bristle tooth," and both angelfishes and butterflyfishes have minute, brushlike teeth. Angelfishes eat mainly sponges, and also algae, tunicates, and zoantharians such as anemones and corals. Juvenile angelfishes have been observed picking ectoparasites from other fishes, but by far the major part of their diet is algae and detritus. Butterflyfishes feed on the tentacles of polychaete worms and zoantharians (Randall). Both fishes are diurnal, spreading over the reefs to feed by day and entering a sleepy state, or torpor, by night, at which time they often exhibit color changes (Randall).

A chief difference between the angelfishes and butterflyfishes is that angelfishes have a preopercular spine, a veritable spike that extends from the gill cover, while the butterflyfishes do not.

Cortez Angelfish (Pomacanthus zonipectus)

photo by Alex Kerstitch

Photo was taken in 30 feet of water at Window Rock off Guaymas, Mexico. Kerstitch used a Nikonos II with flash, No. 26B blue bulb, and Ektachrome X film. Shot at 1/250 second at f/5.6, 3 feet from the subject.

Other differences between angelfishes and butterflyfishes can be seen by looking at the profiles of the two. Butterflyfishes have more pointed snouts and are generally smaller (a notable exception being the small angelfishes of the genus *Centropyge*, the most speciose of pomacanthids). The average size for a butterflyfish ranges between 4 and 8 inches; angelfishes are 12 to 14 inches in length (if *Centropyge* is not considered).

The main genera of the angelfishes are *Holacanthus*, *Pomacanthus*, and *Centropyge*. The *Holacanthus* tend to be the most brightly colored. The species of the *Centropyge* are small, growing to 3 or 4 inches, whereas *Holacanthus* and *Pomacanthus* reach lengths of 2 feet or more. The Indo-Pacific *Pygoplites* is represented by only one species.

The largest genus within the Chaetodontidae is the *Chaetodon*, and most of the butterflyfishes represented in this book belong to this classification. Other genera in the butterflyfish family include *Prognathodes* in the western Atlantic, a counterspecies of *Forcipiger* in the Indo-Pacific; these are the butterflyfishes that have extremely long, tubular snouts well adapted for picking organisms from narrow cracks in the reef. *Chelmon* is another Indo-Pacific genus that features an elongated snout.

Butterflyfishes exhibit important physical characteristics that are vital to their natural means of defense. Almost all of them have a stripe through the eye, and many have a dark blotch near the tail. It is speculated that these serve as a camouflage, and that predators calculating the movement of the butterflyfish by the position of the eye often mistake the posterior spot for the real eye (the real eye being concealed by the stripe). As a result they lunge for the wrong end of the fish. The Foureye Butterflyfish *(Chaetodon capistratus)* may be the best example of this characteristic, although these camouflage markings are fairly strong on all butterflyfishes. Butterflyfishes can also swim backward, which helps in moments of danger. Butterflyfishes have other means of defense besides camouflage. The high bodies and stout dorsal and anal spines deny them as prey to all but the largest predators (Randall), and they can also wedge themselves into an inaccessible, narrow crack in the reef.

French Angelfish

(Pomacanthus paru)

general remarks

Black and glittering with gold-tipped scales, the French Angelfish is one of Nature's supreme underwater works of art. This and the Gray Angelfish *(P. arcuatus)* are the only representatives of the genus *Pomacanthus* in the Caribbean, and both have a regal appearance and stately behavior. Their juvenile forms are nearly identical—black with yellow bars. The two angelfishes are among the most trusting of fishes and readily approach divers (Randall).

physical characteristics

The French Angelfish is primarily black, with the scales tipped with gold. The preopercular spine that distinguishes angelfishes from the closely related butterfly-fishes is also yellow. The face is blue-black and the mouth is white. There is a bright-yellow spot at the base of the pectoral fin. The fish is large, although not quite as large as the Gray Angelfish. It grows to 14 or 16 inches, whereas the Gray Angelfish grows to almost 2 feet.

growth cycle

The juveniles of both French and Gray Angelfishes (about 1 to 3 inches in length) are nearly identical. Both are jet-black fishes with five vertical bright-yellow bands over the body. The primary difference between the two species is in the markings of their tails. The black area in the tail of the French Angelfish is much rounder and larger than the same area in the Gray Angelfish, in which the spot is narrower and more elongated. As the French Angelfish grows, the yellow bands begin to fade and the scales become tipped with gold crescents. The dorsal and anal fins develop elongated filaments that trail behind the fish, and the dorsal filament is yellow. Quite often French Angelfishes are seen in middle stages of the pattern change, with the golden crescents of the body appearing over fading yellow bands.

family, range, and diet

The French Angelfish is a member of the family Pomacanthidae, which is represented in the Caribbean by three genera: *Pomacanthus, Holacanthus,* and the smaller *Centropyge.* The French Angelfish has been recorded on both sides of the Atlantic; in the west Atlantic it ranges from the Bahamas and Florida to southeastern Brazil (Böhlke & Chaplin). It is a solitary fish that is usually seen gracefully gliding near the shelter of the reef, stopping occasionally to pick at sessile marine life. It is diurnal, feeding by day and entering a state of sleepy suspension at night. The French Angelfish is an omnivore, feeding primarily on sponges, and also algae, zoantharians, tunicates, gorgonians, hydroids, and bryozoans (Randall). Juvenile French Angelfishes act as part-time cleaners, picking off ecto-parasites from other, bigger fishes.

photo by Jack McKenney

Photo was taken in 10 feet of water off Grand Bahama Island. McKenney used a Rolleimarin camera with a No. 2 close-up lens, AG1B bulb, and Ektachrome X film. Shot at 1/125 second at f/8.

drawing: Juvenile

Gray Angelfish

(Pomacanthus arcuatus)

general remarks

The graceful Gray Angelfish is the largest of the Caribbean angelfishes, reaching a length of almost 2 feet. It is almost identical in shape and profile to the French Angelfish—large, pancake thin, deep-bodied, with trailing dorsal and anal fins. It swims slowly, stopping to pick off algae and sponges from the reef, and in its own curious way it often investigates divers.

physical characteristics

This big angelfish is basically gray with scales that are edged in light brown, the larger scales having dark brownish-gray spots in the center. The dark spots give the fish its velvety appearance. The inner surfaces of the pectoral fins are yellow. The tail has a light border, and the mouth is white. Like the French Angelfish, the dorsal and anal fins extend into long, trailing filaments.

family and range

The Gray Angelfish is a member of the family Pomacanthidae, represented in the Caribbean by just six species: two in the genus *Pomacanthus,* three in *Holacanthus,* and one in *Centropyge.* The *Pomacanthus* comprise the larger angelfishes and include the French Angelfish and the Gray Angelfish. The Gray Angelfish ranges from New England to southeastern Brazil, including the Gulf of Mexico (Böhlke & Chaplin). It is common in the West Indies, where it is known as the least wary of reef fishes.

diet

Sponges comprise the major part of the Gray Angelfish's diet (as much as 70 percent in some locations), although sometimes the larger part of its diet consists of algae. The Gray Angelfish also eats tunicates, zoantharians, gorgonians, hydroids, and bryozoans. The juvenile Gray Angelfishes act as occasional cleaners, picking off parasites from other larger fishes. Like the French Angelfish, the Gray Angelfish is diurnal, feeding over the reefs by day and entering a state of sleepy suspension at night.

growth cycle

The juvenile Gray Angelfish is so similar to the juvenile French Angelfish that they are very difficult to tell apart. Both are highly desired aquarium fishes, because they are interesting to watch as they adopt their adult color patterns. The juvenile Gray Angelfish is jet black with five bright-yellow bars which fade as the fish grows and takes on the gray pattern. The chief difference between the juveniles of the two species is in the black marking on the tail. The dark spot on the tail of the Gray Angelfish is small and rectangular, while the same spot in the French Angelfish is larger and rounder. As the Gray Angelfish matures, the rectangular spot on the tail spreads until only the light portion is that of the margin at the tip. The fish retains the yellow and black color pattern until it reaches about 4 inches in length, at which time the bars begin to fade and the black becomes silvery gray. The bar that passes under the pectoral fin remains the longest into adulthood. Some 10-inch individuals that have turned gray still have a vestige of this bar.

photo by Bob Cunningham

Photo was taken in 25 feet of water on Molasses Reef in Florida's John Pennekamp Park. Cunningham used a Nikonos camera with 28mm lens and strobe and Ektachrome X film. Shot at 1/60 second at f/11.

drawing: Juvenile

Family Pomacanthidae
Angelfishes

Queen Angelfish

(Holacanthus ciliaris)

general remarks

The Queen Angelfish is so named because of its "crown," the dotted black spot on its forehead ringed in bright blue. The fish is probably one of the most brightly colored fishes of the Caribbean and is distinguished from the look-alike Blue Angelfish because of this crown.

physical characteristics

This is a brightly-colored fish that is basically a vivid blue or blue-green with the scales rimmed in yellow. The pectoral fins and tail are entirely yellow, a feature that distinguishes the Queen Angelfish from the similar Blue Angelfish, the fins of which are only outlined in yellow. The "crown" of the Queen Angelfish is very definite. In the Blue Angelfish this spot is very indistinct.

growth cycle

The juvenile Queen Angelfish is a spectacular little fish that is highly prized by aquarists. It has five vertical blue bars—three on the body and two bordering the eyes. There is no crown. The body is olive with yellow on the forward underside, and the tail is yellow. As the fish grows, the bars increase and then fade, and when it reaches a length of about 4 inches the fish usually has completely adopted the adult color pattern. The Queen Angelfish reportedly reaches 18 inches in length, but more often it attains 12 or 14 inches.

family, range, and diet

The Queen Angelfish ranges throughout the tropical west Atlantic and from the Bahamas to Brazil, including the southern Gulf of Mexico and the Gulf coast of Florida. It is a solitary fish and most often will be seen picking its way along the reef. Divers report Queen Angelfishes being more wary than the French or Gray Angelfishes, and thus they are more difficult to hand-feed. The diet of the Queen Angelfish consists mostly of sponges (96 percent), and also some algae, tunicates, hydroids, and bryozoans (Randall). Juvenile Queen Angelfishes feed more on algae, and like other juvenile angelfishes, they are known to pick parasites from other larger fishes.

family

The Queen Angelfish belongs to the family Pomacanthidae, which is characterized by a sharp preopercular spine. On the pictured specimen this spine is visible in bright blue just in front of the yellow pectoral fin.

photo by Jack McKenney

Photo taken off Freeport, Grand Bahama Island, in 60 feet of water. McKenney used a Rolleimarin, No. 5 blue bulb, and Ektachrome X film. Shot at 1/125 second at f/16.

drawing: Juvenile

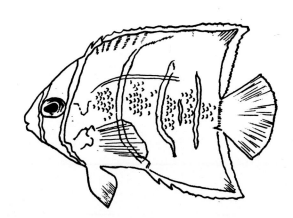

Rock Beauty

(Holacanthus tricolor)

general remarks

The Rock Beauty is an angelfish of the tropical western Atlantic distinguished by its bright yellow and black pattern. The brilliant markings make the fish easy to identify, since there is no other fish in the area with the head, forward part of the body, and tail bright yellow and the rear portion of the body jet black.

growth cycle

The metamorphosis of the Rock Beauty from a juvenile of less than an inch long to a full-grown adult of about 1 foot is an interesting process. The fish starts out solid yellow with a small but prominent black spot just underneath the rear part of the dorsal fin. The black spot spreads as the fish grows, and when the fish reaches about 1½ inches in length, the black covers a major part of the body to the base of the pectoral fin. Finally, at about 6 inches the Rock Beauty is almost entirely black, with only the head, belly, and tail of the fish yellow.

family and range

The Rock Beauty is a member of the Pomacanthidae, which is divided into three genera: *Pomacanthus, Holacanthus,* and *Centropyge.* The fish belongs in *Holacanthus,* along with the Queen Angelfish and Blue Angelfish, and it is the most common of the genus on the West Indian Reefs. The Rock Beauty ranges from Georgia and Bermuda to the Bahamas and southeastern Brazil. It is common off Florida and the Florida Keys.

habits and diet

Like all angelfishes, the Rock Beauty is diurnal. It feeds mostly on sponges, but also on zoantharians and algae (Randall). It is a solitary fish, swimming along the reef and hiding in protective crevices at any sign of danger. The Rock Beauty appears to be more easily frightened than other larger angelfishes, and because of this aquarists are advised to provide the fish with sufficient shelter.

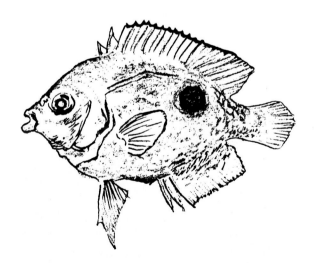

photo by Bill DeCourt

Photo taken at Palancar Reef, Cozumel, Mexico, in 65 feet of water. DeCourt used a Bronica camera equipped with a 75mm Nikor lens, a No. 2 close-up lens, a strobe, and Ektachrome X film. Shot at 1/60 second at f/16.

drawing: Juvenile

Potter's Angelfish

(Centropyge potteri)

general remarks

In the early 1900s a new species of fish emerged from the anonymity of Hawaiian reefs and became known to ichthyologists the world over. The fish was an angelfish and was presented to the U.S. National Museum in 1911 by Frederick Potter, long-time director of the Waikiki Aquarium in Honolulu. Subsequently the new fish was named after him. Today the Potter's Angelfish is a most popular and well-known fish to Hawaiian divers and aquarists around the world. It is very common around all of the Hawaiian islands, yet it is not found anywhere else in the world.

physical characteristics

The first descriptive paper on the Potter's Angelfish, written by D.S. Jordan and C.W. Metz in 1912, described the fish as "one of exquisite delicacy and coloration." The numerous alternating dark and light bars of russet-orange and dark blue immediately distinguish this fish from all other Hawaiian fishes. This pattern is more pronounced on the head and back, and the overall color

appears more orange to the front and darker toward the back. As is typical for the *Centropyge,* the juveniles are not different from the adults and acquire the characteristic pattern soon after leaving the larval stage. In other genera adult angelfishes look very different from the juveniles. The Potter's Angelfish is a relatively small species, reaching about 4 inches in length.

habits and diet

Divers most likely will see the Potter's Angelfish on shallow reefs less than 60 feet deep. The fish is solitary in habit and therefore most likely will be seen by itself. It usually stays close to a coral reef, but sometimes it wanders through rocky areas where it forages for food. The main diet of the Potter's Angelfish consists of benthic algae and detritus, which it picks up with its small

mouth and fine brushlike teeth. In an aquarium it eats almost anything, including brine shrimp and algae, and for this reason is a popular fish among fish hobbyists.

family

Centropyge is one of three major genera of the angelfish family Pomacanthidae. The species within this genus are smaller than other angelfishes (*Pomacanthus, Holacanthus*). Also, *Centropyge* has several additional smaller spines just in front of and below the eye (these are called preorbital spines) which point to the tail of the fish. The Potter's Angelfish was originally described as *Holacanthus potteri.*

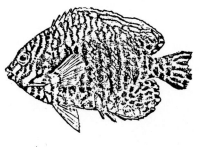

photo by Warren S. Knight

Photo was taken in 25 feet of water off Diamond Head, Oahu, Hawaii. Knight used a Rolleimarin camera with an f/3.5 lens, Honeywell strobe, and Ektachrome X film. Shot at 1/30 second, f/16, 3 feet from the subject.

Clarion Angelfish

(Holacanthus clarionensis)

general remarks

Three species of "Peces angels" are found in the Sea of Cortez (Gulf of California): the Cortez Angelfish *(Pomacanthus zonipectus)*, King Angelfish *(Holacanthus passer)*, and Clarion Angelfish *(H. clarionensis)*. As in the other oceans of the world, these three Mexican angelfishes are spectacular reef inhabitants, their bright colors accentuating their big pancake shapes. The Clarion Angelfish is not as common as the other two species. Scientists D. Thomas, L. Findley, and A. Kerstitch report it off Cabo Pulmo (the tip of Baja), but it is most abundant off Clarion Island, a tiny, uninhabited rock that is part of the Revillagigedo Archipelago. This remote group of three islets is about 400 miles south of Baja and 420 miles east of mainland Mexico.

physical characteristics

The coloration and markings of the Clarion Angelfish are distinctive. The fish is a brilliant orange with a dusky olive face. The tail is bright orange. An iridescent blue forms a rim on the dorsal and anal fins. As is the case with most angelfish species, the juvenile is quite different from the adult. The young Clarion Angelfish is orange with a series of vertical black bars over its body, with two vertical black bars forming a striped effect at the eye. It looks very similar to the young King Angelfish except that the markings of the immature King Angelfish are blue instead of black.

family, diet, and habits

The Clarion Angelfish is a member of the Pomacanthidae, and it eats sponges, algae, tunicates, and zoantharians. Like all angelfishes, the Clarion Angelfish is diurnal, spreading out to feed on the reefs by day and entering a sleepy state by night.

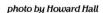

photo by Howard Hall

Photo taken in 40 feet of water off the Socorro Islands. Hall used a Nikon F with a 55mm macro lens in a Farallon/Oceanic Hydro 35, two SR2000 strobes, and Kodachrome 64 film. Shot at f / 8 at 1/60 second, 18 inches from the subject.

drawing: Juvenile

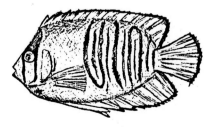

Foureye Butterflyfish

(Chaetodon capistratus)

general remarks

It has been said that nature takes care of its own, and a fine example of this is the Foureye Butterflyfish. This fish has a prominent, large, round ocellated spot near the tail that serves as a "false eye." Confused predators calculate the movements of this fish by this "eye" and consequently may miss their prey. In addition, the real eye of this fish, which normally would be difficult to conceal, is camouflaged by a black band. The Foureye Butterflyfish gets its common name from this false-eye characteristic, because of all the butterflyfishes that have these camouflage markings, this fish may have the most pronounced false-eye spot.

family and diet

The Foureye Butterflyfish is a member of the Chaetodontidae, which includes all of the butterflyfishes. They often swim in pairs along coral reefs. The Foureye Butterflyfish feeds mainly on tubeworm tentacles, sea anemones, and coral polyps (Randall).

physical characteristics

Most chaetodonts have a stripe through the eye and a round spot or marking near the tail, but the physical characteristics of the Foureye Butterflyfish are distinctive. The bold "eye" spot near the tail is black encircled by a bright-white ring. The band through the eye is dark to black with a thin yellow margin. The body of the Foureye Butterflyfish is pale yellow to light gray, the top (dorsal) section of the fish being somewhat darker and more pronounced than the bottom (ventral) section. The pelvic fin is yellow. The body of the Foureye Butterflyfish is thin and disc-shaped and is marked by two sets of thin, diagonal, dark bars that follow the scales and meet in the middle of the body. Across the dorsal and anal fins and extending through the tail are sets of continuous, fine, dark lines. The lines are black with the areas between them a dusky yellow. The tail has a somewhat colorless margin and is rounded. The profile of the upper part of the head is steep, slanting upward to meet the set of jagged dorsal spines on the top of the body.

growth cycle

The Foureye Butterflyfish reportedly reaches 6 inches in length, but it usually averages about 4 inches. The juvenile differs from the adult in that it has another smaller spot above the "false eye" spot, the smaller spot disappearing with age. The young Foureye Butterflyfish tends to be more solitary than the adult.

range

This is the most common of the butterflyfishes in the West Indies. It is found in the tropical Atlantic and Caribbean, including the Gulf of Mexico. It is very common off Florida, and stragglers can be seen as far north as New England, notably off Cape Cod, Massachusetts (Böhlke & Chaplin). On occasion Foureye Butterflyfishes swarm in large groups, creating a spectacularly beautiful sight in the underwater seascape.

photo by Ed Zimbelman

Photo was taken in approximately 50 feet of water outside the reef of Cayman Kai Resort on Grand Cayman Island. Zimbelman used a Rolleimarin with Ektachrome Professional film, and a No. 5 bulb. Shot at 1/500 second at f/8.

drawing: Juvenile

Banded Butterflyfish

(Chaetodon striatus)

physical characteristics

The Banded Butterflyfish is a striking black and white fish, the only chaetodontid in the Bahamas with four dark bars on its body in the adult phase. The adult has no spot, but there may be a slight tinge of yellow on the nose, base of the tail, and top of the head. The juveniles have one spot on the dorsal near the tail, but this disappears as the fish grows older. The juvenile of *C. capistratus* (Foureye Butterflyfish) looks very much like the juvenile *striatus,* but it has two prominent spots where the Banded Butterflyfish only has one. The fish grows to approximately 6 inches in length.

range, habits, and diet

Next to *C. capistratus,* the Banded Butterflyfish is the most common of the Bahaman chaetodontids. It occurs in the east Atlantic, and in the west Atlantic from New Jersey to southeastern Brazil, including the Gulf of Mexico (Böhlke & Chaplin). Divers most often see these fishes singly or in pairs, but almost never in schools. Butterflyfishes in pairs stay very close together as if connected by a rubber band. If one swims ahead, the other hurries to catch up. They are wary fishes and will often dash into a crevice at any sign of danger. They always stay close to shelter, picking about for polychaete tube worms, coral polyps, and anthozoans, which comprise their main diet. They are busy during the daylight, and at night they enter a state of torpor.

photo by Peter Capen

Photo taken in 60 feet of water on Cozumel's Palancar Reef. Capen used a Rolleimarin with a No. 2 close-up lens, a Honeywell 810 strobe, and Ektachrome X film. Shot at 1/125 second at f/22, 18 inches from the subject.

drawing: Juvenile

Milletseed Butterflyfish

(Chaetodon miliaris)

general remarks

Every now and then a diver will be lucky enough to swim into a school of brightly colored, photogenic fishes that will easily accept the presence of a human. It is even better if the fishes will accept handouts and follow the diver in hopes of getting something more to eat. Hawaii's Milletseed Butterflyfish is known for doing this, thereby earning itself the reputation of being the friendliest fish on the reef. In exchange for a few crackers, big schools of them will swarm about the camera, nibbling and picking at divers even when the food has run out.

physical characteristics

The Milletseed Butterflyfish (sometimes called Lemon Butterflyfish) is one of the most common fishes of Hawaiian waters. It is easily distinguished by its bright lemon-yellow body, which is accented by about 11 vertical rows of dark-blue spots that give the fish its "milletseed" appearance *(miliaris* means "milletseed"). In keeping with the common butterflyfish characteristics, the Milletseed Butterflyfish, or "lauwiliwili" as it is called in the Hawaiian Islands, has a dark stripe through the eye and a dark blotch near the tail.

diet

The diet of the Milletseed Butterflyfish includes plankton, small bottom-dwelling shrimp, sponges, and worms. Juveniles of 2 to 3 inches in length have been known to pick parasites from other larger fishes, gaining food for themselves and providing a valuable cleaning service for the host fishes. The fish grows to a length of 6 inches.

range

The Milletseed Butterflyfish is endemic to Hawaii. The related *C. guentheri* (found from Japan to Australia) and *C. dolosus* (in the waters of East Africa) account for erroneous reports of *miliaris* outside Hawaii.

photo by Carl Roessler

Photo taken in 40 feet of water off the Kona Coast of Hawaii. Roessler used a Nikon F camera with a 55mm lens, a Bauer strobe, Kodachrome II film. Shot at 1/60 second, f / 11, 15 inches from subject.

Raccoon Butterflyfish

(Chaetodon lunula)

general remarks

In Hawaii there is a gold and black fish that looks like the masked bandit of underwater reefs. This is the Raccoon Butterflyfish, appropriately named because the black and white eye costume is so reminiscent of the land mammal of the same name. There are other names for this fish: Red-striped Butterflyfish and Masked Butterflyfish. The name "Red-striped" refers to the series of brownish-orange lines that cross the fish backward and upward from the pectoral region. In Hawaii the name for the Raccoon Butterflyfish is kikakapu (kika, "strong"; kapu, "taboo"). In early times many butterfly-fishes were called this, and there are indications that these fishes were considered sacred.

growth cycle

The juvenile Raccoon But-terflyfish is quite different from the adult. Young individuals about 2 inches long have a prominent round, white-ringed spot on the dorsal fin in addition to the black saddle on the tail. By the time they reach about 5 inches in length, this spot has faded into an indistinct vertical bar that rims the base of the dorsal fin. The Raccoon Butterflyfish grows to about 7 inches.

range, diet, and habits

The Raccoon Butterflyfish is an extremely common fish around the Hawaiian Islands and is widely distributed over a good part of the Indo-Pacific. It is found off Australia, Zanzi-bar, and Mauritius, through the East Indies, along China, and through Melanesia, Mic-ronesia, and Polynesia as far as Hawaii. These fishes live in shallow water, often in pairs, and as they cruise about the reefs they pick at algae, coral polyps, and small inverte-brates. The pairing off of but-terflyfishes is apparently a lasting arrangement, and although it is not known whether this is a mating situation or if the fishes are even male and female (this is only suspected from limited data), once they have formed the partnership they rarely stray far from each other. While one swims forward, the other might stay behind a bit but always hurries to catch up.

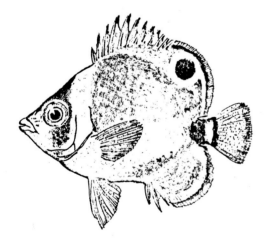

photo by Carl Roessler

Photo taken in 30 feet of water off the Kona coast. Roessler used a Nikon F camera with 55mm lens, a Bauer strobe, and Kodachrome II film. Shot at 1/60 second, f/11, 15 inches from the subject.

drawing: Juvenile

Threadfin Butterflyfish

(Chaetodon auriga)

physical characteristics

The Threadfin Butterflyfish is a common Indo-Pacific reef fish quickly identified by a long filamentous dorsal ray that trails beyond the tail of the fish. In some places the fish is referred to as the "Filament Butterflyfish," although this is not the only species with this filament (Randall). This fin is not fully developed in the juveniles. Another prominent feature: two sets of dark bands that meet at a right angle near the middle of the body. This species also has a moderately elongated snout. The narrow tubelike mouth is well adapted for feeding in the cracks and holes in the reef. The fish grows to about 6 inches, although some reports indicate a maximum length of up to 9 inches.

range

The Threadfin Butterflyfish has been familiar to ichthyologists since it was first reported in 1775 in the Red Sea. It is also familiar to divers since it is found in many of the popular diving spots of the Indo-Pacific region. The Threadfin Butterflyfish is common around the Hawaiian Islands and is found off Australia and Tahiti, throughout the East Indies, Melanesia, Micronesia, and Polynesia, and in the Red Sea. In Hawaii it is sometimes called the Golden Butterflyfish, or "Kapuhili."

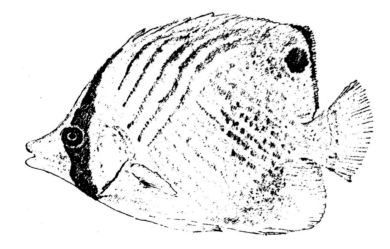

photo by Carl Roessler

Photo was taken in 30 feet of water off Majuro Atoll in Micronesia. Roessler used a Nikon F camera with a 55mm lens, a Bauer strobe, and Kodachrome II film. Shot at 1/60 second at f/8, 24 inches from the subject.

drawing: Juvenile

Beaked Coralfish

(Chelmon rostratus)

physical characteristics

The Beaked Coralfish is one of the most photogenic fishes of the Indo-Pacific reefs and is one of the butterflyfishes with an extremely elongated snout. The fish is yellowish-white with four to five orange, vertical bands, the first three rimmed in brown and the last in pale blue. Within the fourth band, on the soft dorsal fin, is a large black spot edged in white. Across the base of the tail is a narrow black band. The soft dorsal, caudal, and anal fins are edged with narrow blue and white intramarginal lines.

family

The vertical bands, notably the one through the eye, and the large eye-like spot on the soft dorsal are characteristic of the butterflyfish family (Chaetodontidae), to which the Beaked Coralfish belongs. All butterflyfishes have pointed snouts, which are handy for picking up tiny invertebrates from normally inaccessible cracks and crevices in the reef. In some butterflyfishes, such as the Beaked Coralfish, the snouts are extremely elongated. The generic name *rostratus* comes from the Latin word meaning "beak."

habits and range

The Beaked Coralfish generally is found in relatively shallow water in nonsurge zones of heavy coral growth. The fish is common in Australia, especially along the Queensland coast, and ranges from the east African coast to the western Pacific. In northern Australia some large individuals lose the third, fourth, and fifth body bars as well as the spot. *Chelmon rostratus* could possibly be confused with *C. muellerii*, a very close relative in Great Barrier Reef waters. *C. muellerii* has a shorter snout, and the vertical body bars are bronze. The Beaked Coralfish grows to about 9 inches in length.

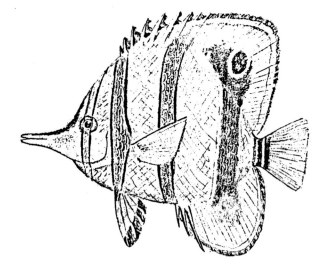

photo by Carl Roessler

Photo was taken in 45 feet of water at Marion Reef in the Coral Sea. Roessler used a Nikon F camera with a 55mm lens, a Bauer strobe, and Kodachrome II film. Shot at 1/60 second at f/11, 15 inches from the subject.

drawing: Juvenile

Damselfishes

(Family Pomacentridae)

Pomacentrids are pugnacious, territorial little fishes which occur worldwide in tropical and temperate seas. Often called demoiselles, and in the Gulf of California "castanuelas," damselfishes look like pug-nosed perches and in some respects resemble the angelfishes and butterflyfishes. They are well known for their brave and feisty behavior. Damselfishes are known to attack intruders many times their size, and territorialism can be particularly evident during mating time, when the male guards the patch of eggs laid by the female. The egg clusters are deposited on hard surfaces such as rocks, dead coral, or pilings. After the eggs are fertilized, the male takes up vigorous watch, swimming back and forth nervously over the potential brood, both to aerate the eggs and to fend off predators. If a diver unknowingly ventures too close to this underwater nest, a fierce little fish will rush out. Some species may even nip at arms, fingers, and fins.

The fishes of the Pomacentridae chiefly are characterized by a single nostril on each side of the snout instead of the usual two. Pomacentrids generally are high-bodied and compressed, except for the species within the genus *Chromis,* which are more elongated and have deeply forked tails. The pomacentrids that are round with shorter, more rounded tails generally live on or near the bottom, while the oval-shaped species with forked tails (the *Chromis*) school in mid-water (Böhlke & Chaplin).

Many juvenile damselfishes have distinctive, iridescent blue spots that gradually disappear with age. The juvenile Garibaldi *(Hypsypops rubicundus),* a bright-orange damselfish of temperate California waters, has the same bright-blue markings as the juvenile Yellowtail Damselfish *(Microspathodon chrysurus)* of the Caribbean.

There are about 275 species in 20 to 30 genera within the Pomacentridae. *Stegastes* (replacing

Beaubrummel (Stegastes flavilatus)

photo by Alex Kerstitch

Photo was taken in 25 feet of water off Manzanillo, Coloma, Mexico. Kerstitch used a Nikon II, 35mm lens, 3:1 extension tube, Subsea strobe, Ektachrome X film. Shot at f/16, 1/60 second, 6 inches from subject.

Eupomacentrus) is the principal New World genus of the Pomacentridae. *Stegastes* is represented in the western Atlantic by a number of species which assume overall dark, drab colors as adults, losing their brilliant rainbow hues to a kind of spreading achromatism that is brought on by age. *S. dorsopunicans, S. planifrons, S. leucostictus,* and *S. variabilis* of the Caribbean and *S. flavilatus* of the Gulf of California all have bright spots and stripes when they are young, but become nearly black, dark brown, or dusky colored as they mature.

The Indo-Pacific genus *Amphiprion* constitutes the anemonefishes or clownfishes—damselfishes that have the ability to live among the stinging tentacles of sea anemones. The stinging cells (nematocysts) of the anemone can instantly paralyze other fishes much larger than *Amphiprion,* but the clownfishes or anemonefishes remain unaffected; the immunity is due to the thicker inert mucous coating or slime of the fish (Lubbock, 1980, Proc. R. Soc. London). The common name "clownfish" is in reference to the bright colors of the fish, usually red with distinctive white bars near the face.

The genus *Abudefduf* includes the sergeant majors of all tropical seas. There are many types of sergeant majors around the world, most of them boldly striped fishes which school almost everywhere within their ranges—in tidepools, grass beds, coral reefs, rock piles, and around wharves and pilings. Like all damselfishes, the sergeant majors are bold and territorial, and they have earned a reputation for being particularly pugnacious. These are hardy fishes that feed both on the bottom and mid-water. During the breeding season the males of some species exhibit a dark-blue phase.

The genus *Chromis* includes a large number of species around the world, including the "Castaneta" *(Chromis atrilobata)* of the Gulf of California, the Blacksmith *(C. punctipinnis)* of the California coast, and the brightly colored *C. cyanea* of the Caribbean. Unlike most damselfishes, which are bottom-grazers feeding largely on algae, the individuals of the genus *Chromis* school mid-water, where they feed on the plankton. The edge of the preopercular margin is smooth in the species of *Chromis* (it is serrated on some other genera, such as *Pomacentrus* and *Stegastes).*

Bicolor Damselfish

(Stegastes partitus)

physical characteristics

In the highly colorful Pomacentridae there is one fish that appears as if it had been held by the tail and dipped into a bucket of paint. This is the Bicolor Damselfish of Caribbean reefs, a fish that exhibits an abrupt difference in color between the front and back parts of its body. The front is essentially a dark black-brown, and the rear is a pale white or pale yellow that extends onto the tail. Of all the damselfishes, the Bicolor Damselfish is said to exhibit the greatest variation in color patterns as an adult. The vertical line of demarcation between the dark anterior and pale posterior sometimes is separated with a bright orange, and sometimes the line extends forward to the tip of the snout, with the pale section reaching the chest. Dr. Alan Emery's studies of the Bicolor Damselfish revealed some individuals that were entirely tan, while others had blue markings. Depth seems to play a primary role in color variations. Böhlke and Chaplin found that individuals from deep water often exhibit larger pale sections. Randall observed deep-water individuals that were blackish at the front and light gray to the back, with the demarcation between the two areas not as sharp as in shallow-water individuals. Most of the anal fin is always dark, the darker area being more pronounced toward the front of the fin. The pectoral fins are yellow with a dark spot at the base of the fins. The color pattern shown here is one that apparently is found on relatively few Bicolor Damselfishes.

life cycle

Most species of the *Stegastes* are highly colorful as juveniles, with a number of spots and markings that are distinctive as to species, and become very nearly black as adults. By contrast, the Bicolor Damselfish does not have any distinct ocelli (spot or line), and there is not much difference between juvenile and adult. Emery records only a very faint blue line in the eye area of the Bicolor Damselfish, whereas there are many brilliant blue markings in most other juvenile damselfishes. The Bicolor Damselfish also differs from others of the genus *Stegastes* in that it has only three rows of scales on the cheek rather than four.

range, habits, and diet

Damselfishes are normally shallow-water inhabitants of coral or rock reefs and sea-grass beds. However, the Bicolor Damselfish has been found at moderate depths. Böhlke and Chaplin report that a Bicolor Damselfish was taken from 40 fathoms in the Tortugas, while another was taken from 200 to 210 fathoms off Puerto Rico. Throughout the West Indies and off Florida the diver most often will see this fish in depths between 25 and 75 feet on isolated patch reefs where it feeds on plant material, small invertebrates, colonial anemones, and worm tentacles.

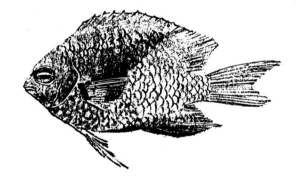

photo by Jack McKenney

Photo was taken in 15 feet of water on the wreck of the Balboa off Grand Cayman Island. McKenney used a Rolleimarin, close-up lens No. 2, Subsea strobe, and Ektachrome X film. Shot at 1/125 second at f / 11, 18 inches from the subject.

Family Pomacentridae
Damselfishes

Sergeant Major

(Abudefduf saxatilis)

general remarks

Sergeant Majors are found circumtropically, and many of them are nearly identical in both behavior and appearance. The Sergeant Major of the West Atlantic *(Abudefduf saxatilis)* is almost an exact look-alike of the Panamic Sergeant Major *(A. troschelii)* of the Gulf of California and the Sergeant Major (maomao) of Hawaii *(A. abdominalis).* In the Western Pacific and Indian Ocean there are Sergeant Majors that are so similar that they were at one time also called *A. saxatilis,* but these species have since been segregated from the west Atlantic species, having a slightly different configuration of the vertical bars and pectoral scales (Allen). In his doctoral studies of *Abudefduf,* Dannie A. Hensley concluded that the Indo-Pacific form is only subspecifically different from the eastern Pacific and western Atlantic forms.

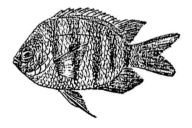

range

The Sergeant Major *(A. saxatilis)* of the west Atlantic is found from Rhode Island and Bermuda to Uruguay, including the Gulf of Mexico. It is an extremely common fish "found everywhere" in shallow water—on coral reefs, in tidepools, grass beds, rock piles, rocky ledges, sandy bottoms, and around pilings and wharves.

physical characteristics

The Sergeant Major exhibits light and dark color phases, depending upon the environment in which it is swimming. In the light phase (over pale, sandy bottoms) the ground color of the fish is gray, sometimes with a greenish tint on the lower part of the body and a yellow tint on the upper part. In the dark phase (over a dark bottom or among deep crevices) the fish can become nearly black, almost entirely obscuring the bars. A similar species, *A. taurus* (Night Sergeant), differs in having much fainter bars, and while the Night Sergeant reaches a length of about 10 inches, the Sergeant Major grows to 7 inches. The Sergeant Major is a much more common fish than the Night Sergeant.

Ichthyologists make the primary differentiation between the two by counting the number of rays on the anal fins. *A. taurus* has only 9 or 10 articulated rays, while *A. saxatilis* has 12 to 13. Also, in the Sergeant Major the mouth is closer to the lower rim of the eye than in the Night Sergeant, a physical characteristic that leads to the defiant, pugnacious look of the fish.

habits and diet

The Sergeant Major is braver than most other damselfishes, swimming more freely out into the open. It is among the most diversified of all fishes in its food habits (Randall), swimming in mid-water to feed on zooplankton and along the bottom to graze on algae or sessile organisms. What it eats is largely dependent upon where it lives. Sergeant Majors that inhabit a reef where algae is abundant can have as much as 100 percent algae in their stomachs, whereas those beneath piers feed mostly on zooplankton or barnacles (Randall). Sergeant Majors also feed on anthozoans, copepods, tunicates, shrimp larvae, fish eggs (of other pomacentrids), and even nudibranchs.

photo by Jack McKenney

Photo was taken in 15 feet of water at the edge of a bluehole between North and South Andros islands. McKenney used a Rolleimarin, Subsea strobe, and Ektachrome X film. Shot at 1/250 second at f/16, 14 inches from the subject.

Black Anemonefish

(Amphiprion melanopus)

general remarks

In the sea there are many cases of interdependency, with one living organism depending upon another for survival and both parties deriving benefits from the relationship. One of the best examples of such interdependency, or commensalism, is the relationship between the Indo-Pacific anemonefish and the anemone. Anemonefishes (or clownfishes) of the genus *Amphiprion* are members of the damselfish (Pomacentridae) that have developed the ability to live among the stinging tentacles of the sea anemone. The anemone provides the fish with an extremely effective shelter, since the fish can dart into the tentacles at any sign of danger, and the anemonefish receives a certain amount of food from the anemone. Some anemonefishes have been observed eating the wastes of certain anemones, as well as food the anemone has regurgitated, and they will also pick off microscopic organisms or slime from the tentacles themselves.

mechanism

In the Indo-Pacific the anemone most closely associated with anemonefishes is the *stoichactis* anemone. The stinging cells (nematocysts) of this anemone would normally paralyze a fish, but the anemonefish has a thick, inert coating of slime (Lubbock) which protects it from the stinging tentacles. An anemonefish that has been segregated from an anemone for a time must reacclimate itself to the tentacles, receiving the desensitizing substance all over again (C. Lavett Smith).

family and physical characteristics

The Black Anemonefish *(A. melanopus)* is one of 27 species of Indo-Pacific damselfishes (Pomacentridae) that have commensal relationships with sea anemones. The Black Anemonefish adult is easily recognizable by its combination of a dusky-black body, bright-orange tail and dorsal fin, and broad blue-white head bar. It has been said that the fish is ill-named because while the blackness of the body is prevalent, the fish is bright orange at the head and throat.

The Saddle Anemonefish *(A. ephippium)* has a similar black region on the body, but does not have the blue-white head bar. The Black Anemonefish grows to 5 inches, while the Saddle Anemonefish grows to only 3 inches.

range and habits

The Black Anemonefish is found throughout the western tropical Pacific, including tropical Australia, Indonesia, Malaya, and the Philippines. The fish typically hangs in suspension over its host anemone while feeding on drifting zooplankton (its main diet), and it never ventures too far from the protection of the anemone. During the spawning season the Black Anemonefish acts like other damselfishes, defending its chosen territory with fierce aggressiveness. When the eggs are deposited, always near the anemone, the behavior of the male becomes almost frenetic. He will fan and pick over the eggs, taking time out only to chase off intruders, including the diver.

photo by Carl Roessler

Photo was taken in 15 feet of water at Marion Reef in the Coral Sea. Roessler used a Nikon F camera with a 55mm lens, a Bauer strobe, and Kodachrome II film. Shot at 1/60 second at f/11, 15 inches from the subject.

drawing: Juvenile

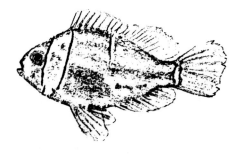

Blue Chromis

(Chromis cyanea)

general remarks

The Blue Chromis is the dazzling sapphire of the west Atlantic reefs. Its deep ultramarine blue, rimmed with black, sets it apart from the small fishes with which it swims, including several species of wrasses and the Yellowedge Chromis *(Chromis multilineata)*. Characteristically, the species of *Chromis* will rise above the reef in large schools to feed upon the plankton, while some of the other damselfish species graze along the bottom.

family, habits and diet

Most species of *Chromis* have elongated bodies and deeply forked tails. The two common species of *Chromis* found in the Caribbean, *C. cyanea* and *C. multilineata*, often swim together and can be separated easily by their colors. Both species appear to feed only on zooplankton, whereas other damselfishes are omnivorous. As the Blue Chromis schools in mid-water, it faces the current to pick up passing plankton from the water mass, primarily copepods, which comprise over 50 percent of its diet. The fish also eats tunicates, shrimp larvae, siphonophores, and fish eggs (Randall). At the first hint of danger the Blue Chromis will instantly vanish into the cracks and crevices of the reef.

physical characteristics

The species name *cyanea* means "blue" (Greek), and the iridescent bright-blue color of the Blue Chromis has been known to vary according to the environment in which it is swimming. The deep blue can fade to a dull grayish blue as the fish reaches the shelter of a reef. In offshore locations where the water is a deep blue, the Blue Chromis has been known to become a brilliant, deep shade, and Böhlke and Chaplin have observed some turquoise individuals. The coloration is possibly a camouflage device (Randall). There is a prominent black margin that rims the spinous dorsal fin and the lobes of the tail. Blue Chromis juveniles look the same as the adults, which grow to about 5 inches in length.

range

The Blue Chromis is a common fish and is most abundant on open and patch reefs at depths between 35 and 70 feet. It has been recorded in waters from 10 to 180 feet throughout the Bahamas and Florida, south through the Lesser Antilles (Böhlke & Chaplin).

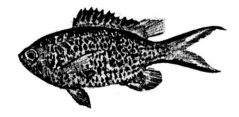

photo by Carl Roessler

Photo was taken in 30 feet of water off Grand Cayman Island. Roessler used a Nikon F camera with a 55mm lens, a Bauer strobe, and Kodachrome 25 film. Photo was shot at 1/60 second, f / 11, 12 inches from subject.

Yellow-Edge Chromis

(Chromis multilineata)

general remarks

The *Chromis* species of the west Atlantic are primarily distinguished by color: brown *(C. multilineata),* blue *(C. cyanea),* and green *(C. insolata).* The Yellow-edge Chromis often schools with the Blue Chromis in mid-water, where they feed on zooplankton. These fishes have elongated, oval-shaped bodies deeply forked tails.

physical characteristics

The Yellow-edge Chromis is olive-brown above, fading to a greenish gray below. Two important identifying marks are the dark blotch at the base of the pectoral fin and the light spot immediately behind the last ray of the dorsal fin. Both of these markings are not present in the Blue Chromis. The dorsal fin of the Yellow-edge Chromis is often rimmed in yellow, a characteristic that

is the source of the common name of the fish. The upper and lower edges of the caudal fin are narrowly yellow, and the tail-fin lobes may be pale yellowish; the pectoral and ventral fins are clear or a pale orange. The shape of the anal fin differs in the two species: in the Yellow-edge Chromis the fin is long and low; in the Blue Chromis it is high and angular (Böhlke & Chaplin). The Yellow-edge Chromis grows to about 5½ inches, and the juveniles look the same as the adults.

family and diet

The Yellow-edge Chromis belongs to the Pomacentridae, in which the generic name *Chromis* has become the accepted common name for some of the species within the genus. The Yellow-edge Chromis feeds on plankton, primarily copepods (87 percent), as well as tuni-

cates, shrimp larvae, siphonophores, pteropods, and crab larvae (Randall).

range

This fish has been recorded in the waters of Bermuda, although this location is questioned, and it also ranges from the Bahamas and Florida, south through the Lesser Antilles (Böhlke & Chaplin). It is most often seen in large schools at depths between 20 and 60 feet, but it has been recorded in open water up to 125 feet.

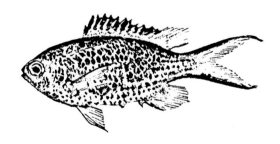

photo by Dick Clarke

Photo was taken in 125 feet of water near a ledge off Grand Bahama Island. Clarke used a Nikon F camera with a 55mm micro lens, and Ektachrome X film. Shot at 1/60 second at f / 11.

Stoplight Parrotfish

(Sparisoma viride)

general remarks

The Spotlight Parrotfish is an excellent example of how individual parrotfishes of the same species can appear very different from one another. The gaudy, terminal-phase male is a blue-green fish with a large bright-yellow spot at the base of the tail, whereas the initial-phase male or female is typically red with evenly spaced white dots. For some time the two phases were considered to be separate species, with the immature phase called the Red Parrotfish *(Sparisoma abild-gaardi).*

physical characteristics

The terminal-phase Stoplight Parrotfish is known for its bright "stoplight-yellow" spot at the base of tail, and there is another small but bright spot of the upper end of the orange-rimmed gill cover. The inner margin of the tail is orange-yellow, and three distinct bands (orange on the very mature individuals) cross diagonally on the head. By contrast, the initial-phase fish has a brownish head and a bright-red underbelly and dorsal fin. The scales of the initial-phase Stoplight Parrotfish are outlined, and there are rows of about five evenly spaced white dots across the body which form a checkerboard pattern. A distinctive white band marks the tail near the base. While many very young parrotfishes look rather nondescript, mottled, or blotched, the Stoplight Parrotfish in its earliest stage is distinctive because even then it has the white-spotted markings. The fish grows to 21 inches, and as it matures, the tail changes from a truncate form in the young, to emarginate in the intermediate stages, to crescent-shaped in the terminal male.

range and diet

The Stoplight Parrotfish ranges throughout the tropical west Atlantic and has been recorded from Bermuda, the Bahamas, and South Florida to Brazil, including the Gulf of Mexico (Böhlke & Chaplin). This is a common fish in the Bahamas, where it has often been seen nipping off chunks of coral rock for bits of algae. Algae comprises almost the total diet of the species (97 percent) but the fish is known to eat a small amount of sea-grasses as well (Randall).

photo by Jack McKenney

Terminal phase Stoplight Parrotfish (Sparisoma viride)

Photo was taken in 60 feet of water off Freeport, Grand Bahama Island. McKenney used a Rolleimarin with Ektachrome X film and a Subsea strobe. Shot at 1/250 second at f / 8, 3 feet from subject.

drawing: Initial phase

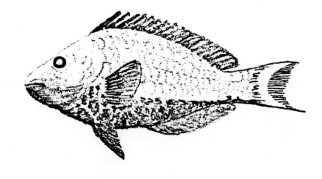

Redband Parrotfish

(Sparisoma aurofrenatum)

physical characteristics

The mature Redband Parrotfish has an orange-red band from the corner of the mouth to just behind the eye, a physical characteristic that is the source of its common name. As in all parrotfishes, the terminal-phase males of the species appear quite different from the immature males and females and are more brightly colored. The terminal-phase Redband Parrotfish is predominantly blue-green with a reddish belly, a yellow-orange spot containing one or two blackish dots on the upper side above the pectoral fin, and dark tips on the caudal fin lobes. The initial-phase males and females are brown or greenish brown with a dark-blue cast on the back and sides, a reddish color in the ventral region, and no yellow-orange spot near the pectoral fin. The initial phase at one time was believed to be a separate species from the terminal phase and was called *S. distinctum.* One marking always present in both phases is the white saddle spot on the base of the tail, a characteristic that provides the best means of identifying the species underwater. The fish reaches a length of 11 inches.

range and diet

The Redband Parrotfish is found from Bermuda, the Bahamas, and Florida to the hump of Brazil, including the Central American coast (Böhlke & Chaplin). It is moderately common and is usually seen swimming by itself over a reef or grass bed, stopping from time to time to nibble at algae or coral rock. Algae forms the largest part of its diet (97 percent) followed by minute amounts of seagrasses, gorgonians, and coral polyps (Randall).

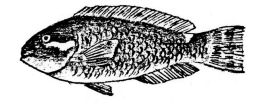

photo by Peter Capen

Photo was taken in 50 feet of water off Grand Cayman Island. Capen used a Rolleimarin camera with a Honeywell 810 strobe and Ektachrome X film. Shot at 1/125 second at f/22, 12 inches from the subject.

Princess Parrotfish

(Scarus taeniopterus)

physical characteristics

The Princess Parrotfish is a species of the family Scaridae and has a colorful terminal male phase. The terminal male, pictured opposite, is a bright blue-green with a broad yellow zone that starts beneath the pectoral fin. There are two narrow blue-green stripes through the eye. *Taeniopterus* comes from Greek words meaning "banded fin"; the dorsal and anal fins of the terminal male are blue with a median orange stripe. The Princess Parrotfish is often confused with the Striped Parrotfish *(S. iserti),* a recent name change from *S. croicensis* documented by Randall and Nelson. Both species have the combination of 3 rows of scales below the eye, 12 pectoral fin rays, and similar markings, but there are distinctions: in *S. taeniopterus* the stripes through the eye are relatively straight, while those of *iserti* are more irregular. The median fins of the two are different: in *iserti* the median orange stripes of the dorsal and anal fins are broader and marbled with blue-green; the caudal fin is blue with a large central region irregularly striped with orange (in *taeniopterus* the orange of the caudal fin is restricted to the upper and lower margins). The initial phases of the two species are even more difficult to separate. The bodies are white with three brown stripes. In *taeniopterus* the upper stripes on either side of the fish unite in a V on the snout, whereas in *iserti* these stripes stop short of the head, rarely extending forward to the eye. Also, the snout of *iserti* is usually yellowish. The tails are different: *taeniopterus* has dark upper and lower margins, while *iserti* does not. *Taeniopterus* is much less common in the Bahamas than *iserti* (Bohlke & Chaplin); it is also a bigger fish, reaching a length of up to 13 inches, whereas *iserti* reaches 11 inches.

habits, range, and diet

Most often the Princess Parrotfish swims along the reef alone, never straying too far from protective shelter. The fish ranges throughout the West Indies and from south Florida to Brazil. Occasional stragglers have been reported as far north as Massachusetts. Like most scarids, the Princess Parrotfish feeds primarily on algae (81 percent) and has also been recorded eating seagrasses and sponges (Randall).

photo by Carl Roessler

Photo was taken in 30 feet of water off Grand Cayman Island. Roessler used a Nikon F camera with a 55mm lens, a Bauer strobe, and Kodachrome 25 film. Shot at 1/60 second at f/ 11, 18 inches from subject.

drawing: Initial phase

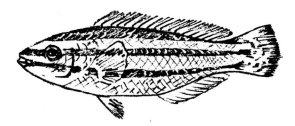

Blennies

(Families Blenniidae, Clinidae/Labrisomidae, Chaenopsidae, Tripterygiidae)

The blennies are blunt-headed, elongated fishes that are bottom-dwellers of tropical and temperate seas around the world. They are believed to be among the most intelligent of fishes; with their big eyes looking out from their hiding holes they appear to be quite alert.

They have strong pelvic fins which are positioned forward of the pectoral fins, and these forward pelvic fins are the chief identifying features of all blennies. With these fins they perch themselves up on a rock, coral branch, or abandoned mollusk shell for a look at their surroundings. The blennies that are carnivorous are ferocious hunters, and when they attack their invertebrate prey, they move so quickly and suddenly that the entire motion can go unseen even to the diver who may be watching. The scaled blennies consist of the Labrisomidae in North and South America and the Clinidae in the Old World; scientists disagree on this classification and often group all scaled blennies in the Clinidae. Clinids and Labrosomids differ from other blennies in having scales on the body but none on the head (except for two species of *Stathmonotus* of the west Atlantic which are entirely scaleless) and in having fixed, conical teeth (they have been called fix-toothed blennies because of this tooth structure). The fourth family, the flag blennies (Chaenopsidae), is sometimes classified as a subfamily of the Labrisomidae. It lacks scales and has no lateral line: the dorsal fin is continuous with about half as many soft rays as spines. The dorsal fin of males of some species is elevated. This group has also been called tube blennies because of their habit of living in various tubes salvaged from deceased invertebrates (Stephens). The fifth family of blennioid fishes is the Tripterygiidae (triplefins), which is distinguished by having a dorsal fin divided into three distinct segments rather than the one (continuous) or two (notched) of the other blennies. Most species of this family are very small.

There are about 600 species of blennioid fishes worldwide distributed among the families. Some blennies are strikingly marked, and almost all of them blend well into their surroundings: tide pools, corals, grass beds, or rocky reefs. Many of them have weedlike cirri growing from their heads—feathery appendages which help to camouflage the fish against a rubble- or algae-covered bottom. Many of the blennies exhibit a wide variation in color patterns. According to Victor Springer, curator of fishes at the Smithsonian Institution, the males of some species can exhibit darker markings than females, and other species can alter their color patterns depending on their emotional states. If frightened, some blennies can become instantly pale.

Blennies are relatively fearless, and divers can get quite close to them to take photographs. Ray and Ciampi report an incident wherein a number of blennies crawled over them, using their pelvic fins for locomotion, and (of the scale-eating blennies who will attack humans) Randall writes: "Their contact is little more than a touch, but when you don't see them coming and believe you are alone on the reef, their little forays can be unnerving."

The behavior of blennies during mating season is similar to that of the gobies (Gobiidae). The male selects the nest and attracts the female by either doing push-ups on the pelvic fins or by bumping her with his nose. When the female enters the nest she goes in tail first, and after the eggs are deposited she leaves the male to guard them. It is during this time that the male blenny exhibits his fiercest territorial behavior.

After the eggs hatch, the young larval blennies, glassy and transparent, drift in the open currents until they reach a shallow, littoral environment, where they drop to the bottom and begin to adopt the steep facial profile and colors of the juvenile. Many post-larval blennies in the past were described as species separate from their adult forms because of the striking physical differences between the growth stages.

Bay Blenny (*Hypsoblennius gentilis*)

photo by Alex Kerstitch

Photo was taken at Isla Tortuga, Baja California, in 40 feet of water. Kerstitch used a Canon F-1, a 55mm macro lens in a Farallon/Oceanic housing, and a Subsea Mark 150 strobe. Shot at 1/60 second at f/22, 8 inches from subject.

Redlip Blenny

(Ophioblennius atlanticus)

physical characteristics

The Redlip Blenny is one of the most common fishes on West Indian reefs. The adult is dark brown and has the typical high, steep, blunt-headed blenny profile. There are single tentacles above each eye. The fish has bright-red lips, the source of its common name, and red markings also appear on the caudal, dorsal, and pectoral fins. There is a dark spot behind the eye, which is another key identifying feature. The young Redlip Blenny is very different in appearance from the adult and was once identified as an entirely different species. It is torpedo-shaped and pale overall. As it grows, the front part of the fish, beginning with the head, becomes dark. Intermediate phases in which the color scheme is half and half are often seen. The fish grows to about 4½ inches in length.

family

The combtooth blennies, family Blenniidae, are characterized by a single series of closely set, comblike teeth and a lack of scales (see introductory remarks for the family). All blennies are blunt-headed and have a pair of pelvic fins in the anterior position. At times the Redlip Blenny has been classified in the genus *Rupiscartes* (Randall). *Ophioblennius* means "snake blenny," which may refer to the elongated shape of the fish.

range

The Redlip Blenny is found throughout the west Atlantic from North Carolina south through the Caribbean and along the Gulf of Mexico and the Central American coast (Böhlke & Chaplin). The fish is known to live in deeper water than some of the other blennies, but its most common habitats are still rocky, shallow places less than 25 feet deep.

diet

Randall has observed that the Redlip Blenny does not bite off large amounts of algae, but rather it scrapes detrital material and fine filamentous algae from rock surfaces. The algae and detrital material comprise 95.5 percent of the diet of the Redlip Blenny, and the rest is composed of a minute amount of fish eggs.

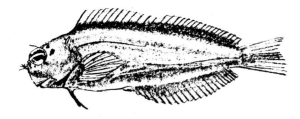

photo by Jack McKenney

Photo was taken in 10 feet of water off Anthony's Key, Roatan, Honduras. McKenney used a Rolleimarin camera, with a Honeywell strobe and Ektachrome X film. Shot at 1/125 second at f/11, 2 feet from subject.

Family Blenniidae
Combtooth Blennies

Diamond Blenny

(Malacoctenus boehlkei)

general remarks

The Diamond Blenny, so called because it is marked with diamond-shaped blotches, is one of four species of the genus *Malacoctenus* that has been observed living with anemones enjoying a symbiotic relationship similar to the anemonefishes (Pomacentridae) of the Indo-Pacific. It is a scaled blenny (Labrisomidae) having a fixed-tooth structure.

physical characteristics

The species of the genus *Malacoctenus* are always strikingly marked and readily identified by color pattern. The Diamond Blenny male has black diamond markings on a pale background of brownish yellow on the head and upper half of the body with a white background below. In the female the diamond markings in the upper row are a brownish orange rather than black, and the lower markings are orange. The ground color of the female is pale orange on the head and upper part of the body; below and between the diamond markings the ground color is white. Both male and female have a black blotch on the forward part of the spinous dorsal fin. The Diamond Blenny closely resembles the Saddled Blenny *(M. triangulatus)*, but in *triangulatus* the dorsal blotch is at the base of the fin rather than slightly above it. While the colors of both male and female are vivid, the Diamond Blenny manages to blend well into its surroundings. Victor G. Springer, curator of fishes at the Smithsonian, points out that blennies are often able to alter their color patterns depending upon their emotional states, paling being a response to a fright situation.

range, habits, and diet

The Diamond Blenny is not a common fish and is known only in the Bahamas and the Virgin Islands (Böhlke & Chaplin), where it lives in a variety of shallow-water habitats. The fish lives on patch reefs and also in corals, on limestone sea bottoms, around coral reefs, and in grass beds. Böhlke and Chaplin found the fish at depths between 25 and 70 feet, with some individuals taken from less than 10 feet of water. Divers have reported seeing the Diamond Blenny within the tentacles of sea anemones. The diet of the fish is believed to be primarily carnivorous, including fish and benthic crustaceans.

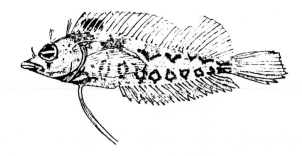

photo by Jack McKenney

Photo was taken in 70 feet of water off Grand Cayman Island, Bahamas. McKenney used a Nikon F with a 55mm lens, an Oceanic 2001 strobe, and Kodachrome II film. Shot at 1/60 second at f/11, 15 inches from subject.

Arrow Blenny

(Lucayablennius zingaro)

general remarks

The Arrow Blenny, a tiny west Atlantic fish which grows no larger than 1½ inches, has swimming habits that have earned it the nickname "slingshot fish." By bending its tail and giving it a quick snap outward, the Arrow Blenny can propel itself forward with a small burst of speed.

physical characteristics

This is one of the flag blennies (Chaenopsidae) characterized by a lack of scales and a lateral line. Of the four species of this family in the Bahamas with protruding lower jaws, only the Arrow Blenny has a protecting fleshy tip on the lower jaw; the tip of the jaw in the others is evenly rounded (Böhlke and Chaplin). The protruding lower jaw gives the Arrow Blenny its pointed, or needlelike, appearance, and it has been suggested that the fleshy tip serves as a lure for the prey it feeds upon (Greenfield). The fish is reddish above, brownish below, and marbled all over. On the soft dorsal fin there are black blotches with pale rings around them, and at the base of the dorsal fin is a golden line which extends the full length of the body. There is a golden streak on the top of the head. The males and females of the species exhibit different color patterns: the male has a dark spinous dorsal fin, while the female is only dark along the base of the fin. In the soft dorsal fin of the male the outer half if black and continuous with blotches. In the female the outer dorsal fin is not so intensely dark and continuous, although the blotches are evident.

habits, diet, and range

The Arrow Blenny is a solitary fish. It lives at depths of between 35 and 70 feet; Böhlke and Chaplin have observed that the fish seems to prefer patch reefs. Like all blennies, the Arrow Blenny spends much of its time sitting inside old worm tubes, burrows, or mollusk shells, propped up on strong pelvic fins to look around for prey; small fishes and benthic crustaceans comprise a large part of the diet. The fish has only been recorded in the Bahamas, Grand Cayman, and Barbados (Böhlke and Chaplin).

photo by Carl Roessler

Photo was taken in 100 feet of water off Grand Cayman Island. Roessler used a Nikon F camera with a 55mm lens, a Bauer strobe, and Kodachrome 25 film. Shot at 1/60 second at f / 16, 12 inches from the subject.

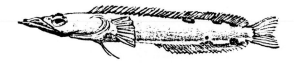

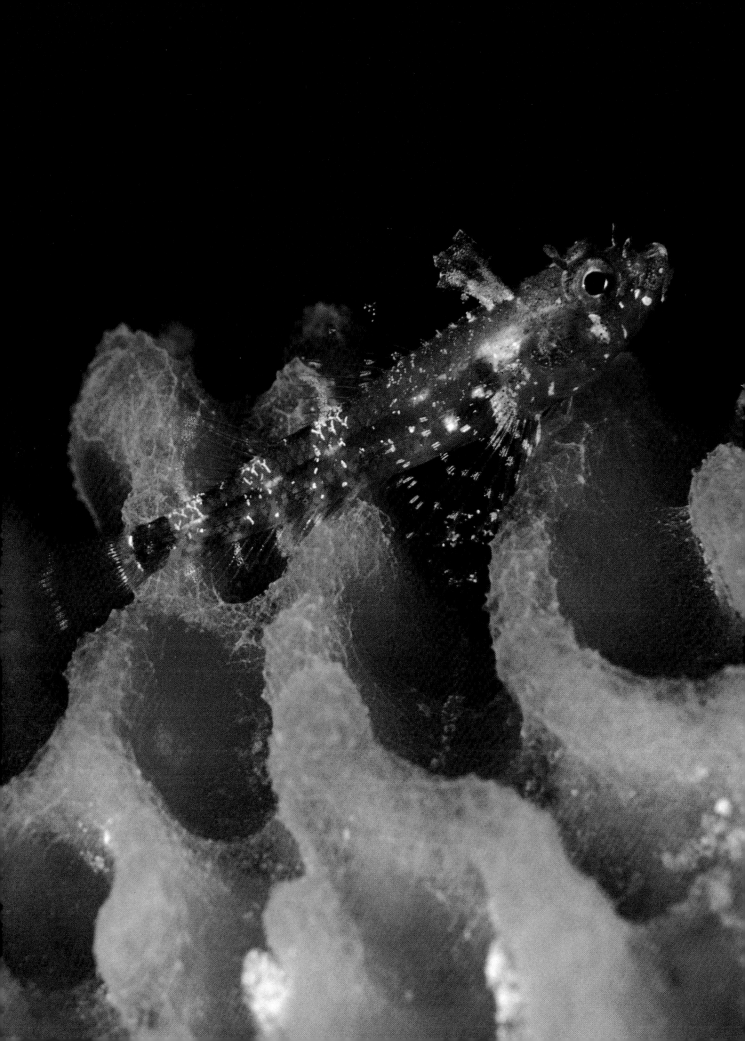

Roughhead Triplefin

(Enneanectes boehlkei)

general remarks

The tripterygiids are distinguished from other blennies in their having dorsal fins divided into three distinct segments. They are all small (less than 2 inches long) and often have five dark bars over the length of their bodies. They are usually found in the protective shelter of a reef, although they sometimes are seen out in the open, foraging for invertebrate food.

physical characteristics

The Roughhead Triplefin grows to 1½ inches in length, looks very much like the Redeye Triplefin (*E. pectoralis*), and most closely resembles the Blackedge Triplefin *(E. atrorus)*. These are basically reddish fishes with different patterns of dark blotches. *E. boehlkei* and *atrorus* are the only species within the genus that lack scales on the belly and pectoral-fin base. *E. boehlkei* has a blunter snout than *atrorus* and a less contrasting color pattern (Böhlke & Chaplin). In the Roughhead Triplefin the body bars are brown, with the last bar, at the base of the caudal fin, the darkest.

range and habits

Böhlke and Chaplin record the Roughhead Triplefin from the Bahamas and Florida to the Lesser Antilles. The two scientists took individuals of the species from patch reefs and from rocky bottoms, never from water deeper than 20 feet and sometimes in just a foot of water. Like all blennies the Roughhead Triplefin stays on the bottom, propped up on strong pelvic fins to view its surroundings and to wait for prey, which consists primarily of small benthic crustaceans.

photo by Paul Humann

Photo was taken in 70 feet of water on the North Wall, Grand Cayman. Humann used a Nikon F with a 105mm lens in a Farallon/ Oceanic housing, and a Farallon/Oceanic 2001 strobe. Shot at f/16, 2 feet from the subject.

Pricklebacks

(Family Stichaeidae)

Decorated Warbonnet

(Chirolophis decoratus)

general remarks

In the north Pacific there are a number of eellike fishes that resemble the blennies and that blend into the bottom so well that the average diver might miss them altogether. These are the pricklebacks—long, skinny, blunt-headed bottom-dwellers that prop themselves up on strong pelvic fins to stare out at their world, which is usually a shallow rock and seaweed place. Pricklebacks are so-called because they look as if seaweed had taken root on top of their heads. These growths are small, plumelike, fleshy protuberances, called cirri, and they extend backward to the first few spines of the dorsal fin.

family

There is one prickleback in which the head decoration is more ornate, and the cirri longer and more weedlike, and this is the Decorated Warbonnet. In the past the fish has been called Decorated Blenny and Decorated Prickleback, and the scientific name of the fish has also changed a number of times since it was discovered in 1809. Today it is *Chirolophis decoratus*, a northern prickleback of the family Stichaeidae. Ichthyologists identify the genus *Chirolophis* by examining the structure of the gill filaments. In all stichaeids the lateral line is single, faint, and marked by a series of minute pores.

range

The Decorated Warbonnet is a solitary fish that has been found at depths between 10 and 50 fathoms off Washington State to northwestern Alaska and the Bering Sea. According to ichthyologists Clemens and Wilby, individuals of the species have been taken in Puget Sound, the Juan de Fuca Strait, English Bay, Burrard Inlet, Stuart Island, Alert Bay, and Prince Rupert Harbor.

physical characteristics and habits

The Decorated Warbonnet is pale brown, or reddish-brown, with irregular white markings overall, a jumble which helps to camouflage it against the bottom. The back of the fish is darker than the belly, and there are prominent dark bands through the eyes and along the dorsal, anal, and caudal fins. The fish has a froglike blenny look, created by thick, turned-down lips. The Decorated Warbonnet primarily feeds on algae and grows to a maximum size of 16½ inches. The pricklebacks are a sedentary group, staying hidden much of the time with only their heads poking out from protective holes in the reef.

photo by Lou Barr

Photo was taken in 70 feet of water at Lena Point, 16 miles north of Juneau, Alaska. Barr used a Nikonos camera with 28mm lens, Subsea strobe, and Kodachrome II film. Shot at 1/60 second at f/16, 3 feet from the subject.

Gobies

(Family Gobiidae)

Bluebanded Goby

(Lythrypnus dalli)

general remarks

California has a few bright, colorful fish that rival the brilliant and showy species found in tropical seas. One of them is the Bluebanded Goby, a tiny, bottom-dwelling creature that stands out from dull-colored, stubby reef growth with its blazing, iridescent red body and equally iridescent blue stripes. The fish is extremely shy, and when a diver approaches it will dart into a hole, crack, or crevice with the speed reminiscent of a retracting anemone. So many Bluebanded Gobies pepper the reefs around Catalina Island, off the coast of southern California, that the fish is often called the Catalina Goby. The scientific name *Lythrypnus* ("red sleeper") is for its bright red color and for its habit of sitting on the bottom. *Dalli* is for the oceanographer W. H. Dall, who discovered the fish.

photo by Howard Hall

Photo was taken in 50 feet of water off San Clemente Island. Hall used a Nikon F-2 with a 55mm Micro Nikkor lens in an Oceanic/ Farallon Hydro 35 housing, two SR2000 strobes, and Kodachrome 64 film. Shot at f / 16.

family and range

The Gobiidae is the largest family of tropical fishes, with about 700 species found worldwide. Forty-three different species are found in the Bahamas, and fourteen off California. Only three species are commonly seen by California divers. The Bluebanded Goby is found from the Gulf of California to Morro Bay, including Guadalupe Island, in waters as deep as 300 feet. More often it is found in shallow, even intertidal, areas.

habits

Gobies are tiny fishes that have no gas bladders and spend most of their time resting on the bottom near a protective hole or crack in the reef. They have strong ventral fins which unite beneath the body to form a sucking disk by which the gobies can attach themselves to a rock, and with this device they can hold themselves in position against the ocean surge. They are ichthyologically separated from the similar bottom-dwelling blennies by the fact that they have two distinct dorsal fins, while the dorsal fins of blennies are single and continuous.

diet and growth cycle

The Bluebanded Goby eats planktonic animals such as gastropods and larval crustaceans, but it also feeds on pieces of seaweed and detritus. The rich plankton currents of California bring food material to the goby, so the fish rarely has to leave its protective spot on the reef to hunt or forage. In spawning, the male goby usually puts on a courtship display for the female, and after she lays her eggs in a protected cave or hole in the reef, the male guards the eggs while they incubate. The male is known to entice other females to lay eggs, to add to the clutch, until he is satisfied there are enough eggs. The juvenile gobies grow quickly, and it is believed that they mature within a few months. The maximum length of the Bluebanded Goby is just 1¼ inches.

Surgeonfishes

(Family Acanthuridae)

Acanthurus comes from two Greek words meaning "tail spine," and it describes a major physical characteristic of the fishes that belong to the family Acanthuridae. Acanthurids—commonly called surgeonfishes, doctorfishes, or "tangs"—have one or more sharp spines near the base of the tail, usually one hinged spine on either side which folds into a horizontal groove or sheath. With one side-swipe of the tail, a surgeonfish can inflict a serious slashing wound to an intruding fish. This caudal knife is the source of the Spanish name for acanthurids, "barberos," since barbers were known to practice bloodletting in early days.

The spines of the surgeonfish are often highly visible, since the sheaths are sometimes brilliantly marked with colors that contrast with the overall body color of the fish. For example, the caudal sheath of the west Atlantic Blue Tang (*Acanthurus coeruleus*) is whitish against blue: in the Yellow Tang (*Zebrasoma flavescens*) of Hawaii the sheath is white against the yellow of the fish. In the Achilles Tang (*Acanthurus achilles*) the caudal spine is enclosed in a large, elliptical bright red-orange spot. This has been cited as an example of warning coloration.

Wounds from the caudal spines of two species of acanthurid fishes have been reported as venomous, the most serious being from the colorful Indo-Pacific *Acanthurus lineatus*. A surgeonfish that gives only a slight side-to-side movement of its tail can send other fishes rushing away.

Surgeonfishes are among the most common fishes of tropical reefs around the world. Some species form large feeding aggregations, and they may graze with parrotfishes over algae-covered corals or rocks. There are about 65 species within the family contained within 6 genera.

Goldring Surgeonfish

(Ctenochaetus strigosus)

general remarks

Known in Hawaii as the "Kole," the Goldring Surgeonfish is unique among the plentiful and colorful assortment of acanthurids represented on Hawaiian reefs. The overall dark color pattern of the fish accentuates its bright yellow eye rings, a characteristic that gave the fish its common name. Island lore about the fish tells us that in ancient times the Kole was tabu to all but the king, who ate it raw and sentenced to death all who took it for their own use.

physical characteristics and family

The Goldring Surgeonfish is one of the most common inshore reef fishes in Hawaii and belongs to the Acanthuridae. The caudal spine of the Goldring Surgeonfish is not brightly outlined as it is in some surgeonfishes and it is difficult to see against the deep brown of the fish.

range and habits

While the Goldring Surgeonfish is extremely abundant in the Hawaiian Islands, it is relatively rare in the rest of the Indo-Pacific. It has been recorded from the Philippines, Moluccas and Celebes, and in small numbers in the Tuamotus and Mauritius. One individual has been recorded from the Great Barrier Reef.

diet

The Goldring Surgeonfish feeds on detrital material, which includes small fragments of filamentous algae and diatoms. Occasionally tiny mollusks, crustaceans, and sponge spicules may be found in the stomach.

photo by Warren S. Knight

Photo was taken in 25 feet of water off Diamond Head on the south coast of Oahu, Hawaii. Knight used a Rolleimarin, strobe, and Ektachrome X film. Shot at 1/30 second at f/16, 3 feet from the subject.

Blue Tang

(Acanthurus coeruleus)

general remarks

In the parade of knife-wielding surgeonfishes (commonly called tangs, since "tangs" are projecting prongs of a knife, fork, file, or sword) the Blue Tang is distinguished among Atlantic species by its deep body, higher counts of dorsal and anal fin rays, and its deep, rich velvety-blue color. The sheath of its caudal spine is white, in sharp contrast to the ground color.

physical characteristics

Of the four west Atlantic species of the family Acanthuridae, the Blue Tang *(Acanthurus coeruleus)* is the deepest bodied (depth $1^7/_{10}$ inches in length without the caudal fin). The Doctorfish *(A. chirurgus)*, Ocean Surgeon *(A. bahianus)*, and Gulf Surgeonfish *(A. randalli)* are more streamlined and do not have such a high dorsal fin. The purple-blue color of the Blue Tang, highlighted by a bright lighter blue on all fins, also distinguishes this species from the other three. Dark longitudinal lines extend the length of its body, whereas *chirurgus* has vertical bars and *bahianus* usually has no marking or only very faint stripes on a brown body. While the caudal knife of the other species is outlined in dark colors, that of the Blue Tang is outlined in white or light yellow, brightly accenting it against the deep color of the fish.

growth cycle

The juvenile Blue Tang appears altogether different from the adult, and in the past it was described as a separate species. It is brilliant yellow, with bright-blue crescents above and below the pupils of the eyes. It keeps this yellow coloration until it is about 3 inches long, although some individuals measuring up to 6 inches have been seen in the bright-yellow phase. At the intermediate stage the Blue Tang is still yellowish, but with bright blue edges on the dorsal and anal fins. In the final stage most of the yellow is gone. It is not uncommon to see a Blue Tang halfway between the stages, with some individuals having dark-blue bodies and bright-yellow tails. The maximum size of the Blue Tang is between 12 and 14 inches. Like all surgeonfishes the Blue Tang goes through a pelagic phase (the late postlarval stage is called the "acronurus") in which it is orbicular, scaleless, and transparent with a silvery abdomen. If ocean currents transport the fish at this stage within the influence of land, it settles down in a suitable inshore habitat and metamorphoses into the recognizable juvenile form.

range, habits, and diet

The Blue Tang is a very common reef fish in the tropical and subtropical west Atlantic, particularly off the inshore reefs of Florida and the Bahamas. It is found from Bermuda to Brazil, including the Central American coast and the Gulf of Mexico, with a few stragglers reported as far north as New York (Böhlke & Chaplin). Like most surgeonfishes, the Blue Tang grazes over open reefs, usually in schools or in the company of parrotfishes, which share similar feedings habits. The Blue Tang has a thin-walled stomach, in contrast to *A. chirurgus* or *bahianus,* which have tough, gizzardlike stomachs. The fish therefore does not ingest much sand and feeds on algae and organic detritus. The crustaceans or coral fragments that an individual Blue Tang might eat are usually the result of an accidental intake as the fish grazes on plant material (Randall).

photo by Jack McKenney

Photo was taken in 20 feet of water on the wreck of the Balboa at Grand Cayman Island. McKenney used a Rolleimarin, Ektachrome X. Subsea strobe. Shot at 1/250 second at f/11, 18 inches from subject.

drawing: Juvenile

Yellow Tang

(Zebrasoma flavescens)

general remarks

Zebrasoma means "zebra body," which is the generic name originally given to the Sailfin Tang *(Z. veliferum)*, a fish that has dark zebra bars on the body. The genus eventually included the brightly colored fish called the Yellow Tang, because it has the same high profile—a deep body and very high dorsal and anal fins with only four or five dorsal spines. These characteristics separate both species from others of the family Acanthuridae.

physical characteristic

The species name *flavescens* comes from the Latin for "yellow," and the bright lemon color of the Yellow Tang is perhaps its most obvious characteristic. The Hawaiian name for the fish, lau'i-pala, means "yellowed ti leaf." The caudal spine, a knifelike weapon for which surgeonfishes are named, is sheathed in white, in contrast to the yellow body. The Yellow Tang is distinguished from other Hawaiian surgeonfishes in having very high dorsal and anal fins and a more elongated snout. The fish reaches a maximum length of 8 inches.

range and habits

The Yellow Tang is one of the most common reef fishes in Hawaii and occurs from near shore to depths of at least 150 feet, most often on reefs dominated by finger coral *(Porites)*. Elsewhere the fish is known only from the Marshall Islands, the Marianas, Wake Island, Marcus Island, and southern Japan (Randall). A close relative of the Yellow Tang, the Brown Tang *(Z. scopas,* which was believed to be a color variation of *Z. flavescens* until Randall determined that the two had slightly different numbers of dorsal and anal fin rays), does not occur in Hawaii. However, the two species live together in some of the tropical Indian and Pacific Ocean locations where their ranges overlap, and occasional individuals that exhibit an intermediate color between the brown and yellow are believed to be hybrids (Randall). The Brown Tang has a much broader distribution, ranging from French Polynesia to East Africa.

diet

Most surgeonfishes graze on benthic (filamentous) algae, and this comprises the main diet of the Yellow Tang (Randall). The fish is one of the most popular aquarium fishes exported from Hawaii, and in captivity it is known to take animal food such as brine shrimp. However, says Randall, it should always be provided with plant material.

photo by John E. Randall

Photo was taken in 6 feet of water in the quarry pool of the windward reef, Eniwetok Atoll, Marshall Islands. Randall used a Nikon F-1 with a 105mm lens and Vivitar 292 strobes, and Ektachrome (ASA 64) film.

Moorish Idols

(Family Zanclidae)

Moorish Idol

(Zanclus cornutus)

general remarks

When an artist is called upon to paint an underseascape, chances are that at least one Morrish Idol will be included. *Zanclus cornutus,* a beautiful fish found in many of the world's tropical seas, is one of the most common fish subjects of artists and designers. It is not hard to see why. It is an extremely graceful and beautiful addition to the subsea reefs within its broad range. It occurs throughout the Indo-Pacific, from East Africa to eastern Oceania, and is one of the few fishes of this region to extend its distribution to the eastern Pacific.

family

The familiar outline of the Moorish Idol—the extended filamentous dorsal fin, the long pointed snout and disk-shaped body—distinguishes the fish from all others. The Hawaiian name for the fish, *kihikihi,* meaning "angular," refers to the steep, pointed look of the head. On the head above the eyes adults develop a pair of bony horns which are larger in males. The name *cornutus* is from the Latin, and refers to these horns. Some physical and behavioral characteristics of the Moorish Idol

are reminiscent of other fish families. Like the butterfly-fishes, the Moorish Idol has brushlike teeth and swims about the reef probing for food (invertebrates and filamentous algae) in cracks and crevices with its long, pointed snout.

growth cycle

Zanclus cornutus reaches an exceptionally large size as a postlarva—up to 3 inches in length. Such a large size means a long period of larval development, which explains how this fish has achieved such broad distribution. The postlarval stage resembles the juvenile. There is a prominent curved spine on the preorbital bone (just behind and above the corner of the mouth); this spine is shed as a unit during transformation to the juvenile stage (Randall). The postlarva was named as different species, *Z. canescens,* by Linnaeus (1758) in the famous *Systema Naturae* (which is the cornerstone of our system of biological nomenclature), but the description is clearly of *Z. cornutus.* Cuvier and Valenciennes were the first to suspect that the two were the same, and they adopted the name *cornutus* for the species. The Moorish Idol reaches about 7 inches in length.

habits and physical characteristics

The diver might identify the Moorish Idol simply by the outline of the fish, but the color pattern is also a distinguishing feature. There are broad black bands on the body, the tail is black and trimmed in white, and the triangular yellow or orange spot on the snout is rimmed in black. The fish usually will be seen individually, but may at times occur in small groups. They are not particularly skittish and will stay around in the general area of the diver. At night the Moorish Idol settles down and apparently sleeps, but it is not as easy to approach them as it is to approach most butterfly-fishes or surgeonfishes.

photo by Carl Roessler

Photo was taken in 35 feet of water off Hawaii. Roessler used a Nikon F camera with a 55mm lens, a Bauer strobe, Kodachrome II film. Shot at 1/60 second at f/11, 15 inches from subject.

Triggerfishes & Filefishes

(Family Balistidae)

Triggerfishes and filefishes are peculiar fishes characterized by tough, scratchy hides, hard-shelled bodies, or prickly spines. All have several jaw bones fused, and instead of overlapping scales there are plates or spines. The triggerfishes and filefishes have a unique spinous dorsal fin: the first dorsal spine is long and stout and in the triggerfishes it can be locked in an erect position.

Triggerfishes (family Balistidae) get their name from this triggerlike dorsal device. There are three dorsal spines. The first one is the largest, and when it is erected, the small second spine moves forward and locks the first in an upright position; it stays locked until the "trigger" spine is depressed. When a triggerfish is threatened, it squeezes itself into a crack in the reef and locks the long dorsal spine into place, thereby wedging itself firmly into its hiding place. The word *balistes* means "cross bow," in reference to this characteristic. The triggerfish is also capable of lowering its pelvic flap, which also helps to lodge it into its hiding hole.

Balistids are believed to be derived from acanthuridlike stock, and the profiles of triggerfishes suggest such a connection with the surgeonfishes: both have deep bodies, eyes set high on the head, relatively pointed snouts, and small mouths. The strong, chisel teeth of the triggerfish are well adapted for crunching through the hard parts of the invertebrates they eat, which include crabs, mollusks, and sea urchins. The scales are hard and platelike, embedded in the skin; they give the fish a tough, leathery feel. The eyes of balistids are unique in that they are capable of moving independently of one another. A triggerfish can keep one eye on a diver or predator while focusing the other on an escape route.

(Family Monacanthidae)

The filefishes (Monacanthidae) are very closely related to the triggerfishes, and some ichthyologists group the two families together. However, there are scientists who make a further separation, singling out *Aluterus* and its relatives from the filefishes into their own family, Aluteridae. The filefishes differ from the triggerfishes in that they have one elongated dorsal spine, with a small second spine that does not function like a trigger as in the Balistidae. Filefishes have more compressed bodies than triggerfishes and scales that are not as pronounced. The scales of filefishes have small spinules—minute spines—which give the fish a rough texture like that of sharks. Sailors of the past often dried the skins of filefishes to hang by their galley stoves to use in striking matches. There is often a patch of bristles, or setae, at the base of the caudal fin of filefishes: this feature is more pronounced in some species (such as *Cantherhines macrocerus*) than others.

Like the triggerfishes, filefishes have the ability to rotate their eyes independently. They are generally shy and secretive; like the trumpetfishes (Aulostomidae) they try to hide among plants, corals, or other reef growths, sometimes vertically aligning themselves next to their hideouts and remaining motionless. Many of the filefishes are capable of instant color or pattern changes; the Whitespotted Filefish *(Cantherhines macrocerus)* may appear a solid orange or gray-brown one minute, then instantly white-spotted the next. Filefishes are not efficient swimmers; their dorsal and anal fins ripple toward the rear to move the fish slowly forward, and the tail fin is rarely used.

The juveniles of some species of filefishes are known to float with sargassum weed or other flotsam in the open ocean, a habit which distributes them far and wide. Their pelagic existence is the chief reason why most filefishes are distributed over a wide range.

Queen Triggerfish *(Balistes vetula)*

photo by Jack McKenney

Photo was taken in 30 feet of water off Conception Island, Bahamas. McKenney used a Nikon F in an Oceanic housing, Honeywell strobe, and Kodachrome X film. Shot at 1/60 second at f/8, 2 feet from the subject.

Sargassum Triggerfish

(Xanthichthys ringens)

general remarks

The Sargassum Triggerfish gets its common name from the fact that the young of this species are often found among clumps of floating sargassum weed. The species name, *ringens,* means "open," or "gaping," and refers to the three grooves on the head of the fish—a characteristic that identifies the species.

physical characteristics

This is only west Atlantic triggerfish that has parallel, black grooves from below the mouth to the area of the pectoral fin; there are three grooves in all. The body can be yellow, green, blue, or violet, blue being most commonly exhibited. The body is spotted, and the spots occur where the scutes intersect to form almost regular rows. The iris of the eye is often red. The bases of the dorsal and anal fins are black, or sometimes red. The caudal fin can be entirely red, or with the upper, lower, and posterior edges scarlet. (Because of this characteristic an early name for the species was Red-tailed Triggerfish.) The Sargassum Triggerfish grows to 10 inches. The stout dorsal spine, a characteristic of all balistids, is sometimes difficult to detect when the fish is lying flat, but on the pictured individual it can be seen on top of the head just behind the eye.

range, habits, and diet

The Sargassum Triggerfish is a west Atlantic species which ranges from Bermuda and South Carolina throughout the West Indies and Gulf of Mexico to Brazil. There are four other species in the genus, all from the Indo-Pacific (one of which also occurs in the eastern Pacific). The Sargassum Triggerfish usually lives in depths greater than 100 feet; Randall notes that the adults of the species are rarely encountered above this depth, but that below 100 feet they are one of the most abundant of West Indian reef fishes. Like most balistids the Sargassum Triggerfish is solitary and shy; it will dart into a crack if theatened, wedging itself into a hiding place by using the trigger-locking device characteristic of the family. The Sargassum Triggerfish has a small mouth, but like all balistids it has powerful jaws and sharp teeth; this enables the fish to feed on hard-shelled invertebrates such as crabs, mollusks, and sea urchins.

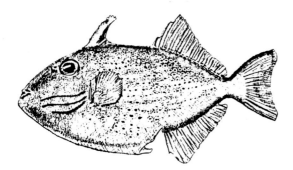

photo by Jack McKenney

Photo was taken in 60 feet of water off Santa Rosa Reef, Cozumel. McKenney used a Nikon in an Oceanic housing, 55mm lens, Oceanic 2001 strobe, and Kodachrome 64 film. Shot at 1/60 second, f/8, 4 feet from subject.

Whitespotted Filefish

(Cantherhines macrocerus)

general remarks

Cantherhines comes from the Greek words for "spine" and "snout," in reference to the anterior position of the first dorsal spine. *Macrocerus* comes from the Greek words meaning "big" and "horn," in reference to the spines, or setae, at the base of the tail. While these spines occur in other filefishes, they are much more pronounced in the Whitespotted Filefish.

physical characteristics

The setae, or spinelike bristly hairs at the base of the tail of the Whitespotted Filefish, differ between male and female; the male has the larger spines. The fish is typically brownish with a bright-orange wash in the tail region, and it is covered overall with white spots that can disappear in moments. There is a pale, triangular saddle on each side of the body. The fish can change the intensity of its coloration at will, sometimes looking almost white and spotless and at other times appearing almost black. This is a defense mechanism that allows the fish to "disappear" before the eyes of predators. Like all filefishes, the rough, shagreen texture of the skin is created by denticulate scales. The Whitespotted Filefish grows to almost 17 inches.

range, habits, and diet

This is not a common fish within its west Atlantic range. It is found from Florida, the Bahamas, and Bermuda to Brazil. It is apparently a relatively shallow-water fish; Böhlke and Chaplin never collected it deeper than 70 feet and have found it in less than 10 feet of water. Randall observed that the fish most often swims in pairs, possibly in male/female combinations. Sponges comprise the main part of its diet (86.5 percent), followed by minute amounts of hydrozoans, gorgonians, and algae (Randall). Like all filefishes this fish is a poor swimmer and will usually be seen nipping and picking its way slowly along the rocks and reefs. It has the ability to move each eye independently, keeping one eye on where it has been and another on where it is going. It is shy and stays close to cover, near rocks or coral crevices, never swimming too far off the bottom. At times it will revert to a straight vertical position to hide next to a sea fan or coral.

photo by Peter Capen

Photo was taken in 40 feet of water off Klein Bonaire. Capen used a Rolleimarin camera, Rolleimarin close-up lens, Hydro strobe, and Ektachrome X film. Shot at 1/125 second at f/16–22, 2 feet from subject.

Longnose Filefish

(Oxymonacanthus longirostris)

general remarks

Oxymonacanthus comes from Greek words meaning "sharp single spine," and *longirostris* comes from Latin words meaning "long nose." These are partial but accurate descriptions of a fish that has the single, sharp dorsal spine for which filefishes are noted, and an elongated snout, which is a feature distinctive to the species.

physical characteristics and range

The Longnose Filefish is basically a little green fish with bright-orange spots. It is small, reaching a length of only 2 or 3 inches; the yellow surrounding the eye is crossed by six radial blue bars, and the bright-orange pelvic flap is marked by an irregular yellow-green pattern over a blackish brown. There is a dark spot on the caudal fin. The fish has been recorded off Australia, through parts of the Indo-Pacific, throughout Micronesia, Melanesia, and Polynesia (except Hawaii), and into the Red Sea. While *O. longirostris* has been the accepted scientific name for the fish, the Red Sea form was recently given a different subspecies name—*O. halli.* According to John McCosker of the Steinhart Aquarium, the Red Sea form differs from the Pacific form by one or two fin rays. Barry Hutchins of the Western Australian Museum in Perth recognizes *halli* in the Red Sea as a valid species distinct from *longirostris,* and while other ichthyologists are following Hutchins, there are those who still regard the two forms as subspecies.

diet and habits

The long snout of *O. longirostris* is well suited to its diet, which consists primarily of coral polyps and sometimes the tiny animals that hide in narrow coral crevices. Because the Longnose Filefish prefers living coral above all else, it is difficult to keep in captivity. There are successful dietary substitutes for the coral polyps, but aquarists must still provide some sort of coral habitat in which the fish can hide. The juvenile of the species is known to float with sargassum weed in the open ocean, hiding among the fronds as it drifts; this is a habit of other juvenile filefishes and is one reason why many of them enjoy a wide range. By the time the Longnose Filefish has reached adulthood, it will have settled down to life in the coral, and studies have revealed that the fish pairs off with a mate, with which it stays faithfully (Barlow).

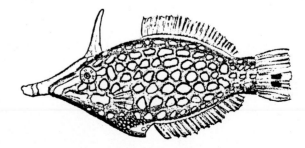

photo by Chris Newbert

Photo was taken in the Red Sea. Newbert used a Canon F-1, 55mm macro lens, Farallon/Oceanic Hydro 35 housing, Farallon/Oceanic 2003 strobe. Shot at ISO 25 at f/16, 10 inches from subject.

Trunkfishes

(Family Ostraciidae)

Spotted Trunkfish

(Ostracion meleagris)

general remarks

The scientific name of the trunkfish family, Ostraciidae, comes from the Greek *ostracum*, which means "shell," and this describes the hard carapaced body of the fishes within the family. *Meleagris* is from the Greek name for a guinea fowl, a bird that has dark feathers speckled with white. Both scientific names describe the Indo-Pacific fish commonly called Spotted Trunkfish ("moa" in Hawaii).

physical characteristics

The large males of *Ostracion meleagris* are much more brightly colored than the females; the top of the body from the eye to the tail is dark brown to black with white spots, the entire dark area is rimmed in brilliant orange-yellow, and the lower part is blue. In Hawaii the side of the body has small black spots Away from Hawaii

photo by Chris Newbert
Photo was taken in 40 feet of water off Kona, Hawaii. Newbert used a Canon F-1 with a 50mm lens in an Ikelite housing with a flat port and an Oceanic/Farallon 2003 strobe. Shot at ASA 25 at f / 16, 1/160 second.
drawing: Female

males have dark-edged orange-yellow spots on the side. The immature individuals and females are uniformly dark brown with white spots all over. (Larger fish have more spots, and those in Hawaii have fewer spots than individuals of the same size elsewhere). The geometrically shaped pattern on the lower part of the fish is created by calcified bony plates that make up the entire carapace. This shell-like armor starts at the nose and stops at the base of the tail, and there are gaps through which the fins protrude. The fish grows to a maximum length of 5 or 6 inches.

habits and diets

Because of its heavy armor and weak fins, the Spotted Trunkfish is a poor swimmer, all movement being confined to the sculling action of the fins and tail. If a diver approaches, the fish will paddle frantically with its pectoral fins, using its tail only as a rudder. While it swims, it rocks back and forth to keep an eye on its pursuer, a type of swimming that is called "ostraciiform movement." The Spotted Trunkfish stays close to the bottom or near a reef, usually in shallow water, where it

feeds on invertebrate animals such as tunicates and worms. Like the Smooth Trunkfish *(Lactophrys triqueter)* of the west Atlantic, the fish is capable of emitting a toxic mucus strong enough to kill other fishes in an aquarium. Professional collectors normally take special precautions when handling the fish, exposing it to stress so that it will secrete the slime, then rinsing it off before placing it in the collecting bucket.

range

The Spotted Trunkfish is the most common of the trunkfishes in Hawaii, where it is regarded as a different subspecies—*Ostracion meleagris camurum. O. meleagris meleagris* ranges from East Africa (but not the Red Sea) to the tropical eastern Pacific (Randall).

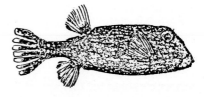

Puffers

(Family Tetraodontidae)

Sharpnose Puffer

(Canthigaster rostrata)

general remarks

This little puffer, like others of the family Tetraodontidae, is an amusing fish which can blow itself up into a round ball. When a predator theatens, or when it is alarmed for any other reason, it sucks water into its abdomen (or air, if it is removed from the sea) and literally puffs itself up to twice its normal size. The fish also has tiny spinules on its body which stand up in their sockets when the fish is inflated.

physical characteristics

The Sharpnose Puffer is the most common puffer of Caribbean reefs. It is also the smallest, reaching a maximum length of 4½ inches. It is a brightly colored fish, the most characteristic markings being the black upper and lower margins of the tail and the iridescent blue lines and markings on the brown body. There is a vertical blue line on the tail, blue lines radiating from the eye, blue lines on the nose, and scattered blue spots elsewhere. All of the fins are orange, and the iris of the eye is also orange. The skin of the puffer is tough, scaleless, and smooth except for tiny spinules on the lower part of the head and abdomen, each one capable of folding back into a small socket *(Canthigaster* comes from the Greek for "spine belly," in reference to this). *Rostrata* means "long-snouted" in Latin, in reference to the relatively long, pointed, sharp nose of the fish. This last characteristic separates the Sharpnose Puffer from all other Caribbean puffers. Its smaller size, bright coloration, and general body shape are also differentiating factors. Other puffers are somewhat cylindrical, while the Sharpnose Puffer is moderately compressed, the profile distinguished by a fleshy ridge or "keel" just before the dorsal fin. Because of its distinctive characteristics, some scientists place the Sharpnose Puffer in its own family, Canthigasteridae. However, the fish is usually included with other puffers in the family Tetraodontidae. *Tetraodont* means "four-toothed," in reference to the beaklike dental plates divided by a median suture.

diet and habits

The Sharpnose Puffer is omnivorous and eats marine spermatophytes (higher plants, including sea grasses), sponges, crabs, shrimps, polychaetes (worms), pelecypods, hydroids, and algae (Randall). The fish can be found from shallow seagrass beds near shore to rock reefs at 100 feet, and from rocky tidepools to deep coral clumps covered with seafans and whips. The puffer has a peculiar manner of paddling along with the rear part of its body curved to one side. It is not a very good swimmer, and to protect itself it relies on its ability to puff itself up into a prickly ball. Although it is often seen alone on the reef, the Sharpnose Puffer is known to band together with other Sharpnose Puffers when danger threatens. These fishes are found on both sides of the Atlantic, and in the west Atlantic they range from Bermuda and Florida to the northern part of South America, including the Gulf of Mexico (Böhlke & Chaplin).

photo by Chris Newbert

Photo was taken in 30 feet of water off Belize. Newbert used a Canon F-1 with a 50mm macro lens in an Ikelite Housing, a Farallon/Oceanic 2003 strobe, and Kodachrome 25 film. Shot at f/16, 15 feet from the subject.

drawing: Inflated state

Porcupinefishes & Burrfishes

(Family Diodontidae)

Spiny Puffer

(Diodon holocanthus)

general remarks

The Spiny Puffer is an inflatable pincushion of tropical seas. In its normal state it is relatively streamlined like other fishes, but when it is alarmed it puffs itself up into a big round ball with the sharp quills projecting outward. This is its natural defense against the larger predatory fishes that would not care to bite into such a mass of spikes. When the Spiny Puffer puffs itself up like this, it can barely swim and becomes an easy target for human curio collectors. Often it becomes ensnared in fishing nets, and a good many are brought up this way. The fish is frequently seen inflated and lacquered in souvenir shops; otherwise, it is of little commercial value. The flesh has been reported as poisonous.

photo by Carl Roessler

Photo was taken in 35 feet of water off Bonaire in the Caribbean. Roessler used a Nikon F camera with a 55mm lens Bauer strobe, and Kodachrome II film. Shot at 1/60 second at f/8, 2 feet from subject.

drawing: Inflated state

family, range, and physical characteristics

The family Diodontidae include the porcupinefishes *(Diodon)* and burrfishes *(Chilomycterus),* which differ in that porcupinefishes have two-rooted spines which can lie flat, while burrfish spines are three-rooted and rigidly erect at all times. *Holocanthus* means "wholly spined," which refers to the spiny body of the Spiny Puffer, a member of the Diodontidae (not to be confused with the puffer family Tetraodontidae). The two most common species of *Diodon* are *D. holocanthus* and *D. hystrix* (the Porcupinefish). Both occur around the world. In the western Atlantic Spiny Puffers are found from Florida and the Bahamas to Brazil, including the Central American coast. In the Bahamas they occur in shallow waters usually less than 20 feet deep, in mangrove-lined tidal creeks, on small patch reefs, in shallow, sluggish canals, and in harbors (Böhlke & Chaplin). They are bottom-dwellers, probably because they are not the best swimmers even when deflated. In the south and eastern Pacific Spiny Puffers are found from the Cape of Good Hope, along India, through the East Indies, the Philippines, along the coasts of China, Queensland, and through most of Micronesia and Polynesia, including the Hawaiian Islands. It seems to be absent from some oceanic islands of the South Pacific, but it is present off Easter Island and Pitcairn.

diet

The word *Diodontidae* means "two toothed," referring to the ichythyological fact that the beaks of the porcupinefishes are not divided by a median suture (which separates them from the puffers). Its powerful jaws enable the Spiny Puffer to crunch through the hard shells of mollusks, echinoids (sea urchins), and crustaceans. Gastropods make up the largest part of the diet, followed by pelecypods, echinoids, hermit crabs, and crabs (Randall).

Molas

(Family Molidae)

Mola Mola

(Mola mola)

family

The Mola Mola belongs to the Molidae, a family that includes three species of sunfishes and headfishes. The other two are *Masturus lanceolatus* (sometimes classified in *Mola)* and *Ranzania laevis.* The Mola Mola is a fish of the open seas and is found off Australia, off both sides of the Atlantic, and in the eastern north Pacific . From time to time it is abundant off California.

The Mola Mola can grow to an enormous size. A record 4,400 pound individual collided with a steamer off Australia . Maximum growth is normally around 2,000 pounds, but off California the Mola Mola will rarely exceed 3 feet in length or 125 pounds.

general remarks

Not many fish are commonly known by their generic names, but "Mola Mola" is a universal tag that has been applied to a very odd fish that occurs around the world. The Mola Mola has been known and loved by sailors and divers who throughout the history have best described the fish as one whose tail has been bitten off. In almost every tropical and temperate sea this fish can be found lying on the surface on its side basking in the sun. At the approach of a boat it will quickly flop away, but before disappearing it will very often leap completely out of the water, slapping its body in a noisy way on the surface as it dives back in. The sun-basking habit of the Mola Mola has earned it the nickname "Ocean Sunfish." There are other names for this sea creature, one of the most common being "Headfish," a reference to the fact that the fish looks like a big floating head. In Hawaii it is called "Makua" or "Kunehi." *Mola mola* is a name given to the fish by the Swedish botanist Linne; "mola" means "mill wheel," a reference to the fact that the fish resembles a circular milling stone.

physical characteristics and growth cycle

The adult Mola Mola is easily recognized by its oval, silver body. The tough leathery hide is scaleless and elephantlike, covered with a slime. The tail fin is scalloped and rather useless in swimming. The fish propels itself with the large dorsal and anal fins which beat alternately back and forth from side to side. At times the fish simply paddles itself around on its side. The juvenile Mola Mola looks quite different from the adult. It is a tiny pea-shaped fish that bristles with spines, or jutting triangular projections. These spines disappear as the fish grows.

diet and habits

The diet of the Mola Mola is as odd as the fish itself—primarily jellyfish, but also ctenophores, crustaceans, small fish, and pelagic mollusks. The fish is heavily infested with tapeworms and other parasites, which is why the California diver will often see it surrounded by a host of cleaner fish such as surfperches or senorita wrasses; it is also why the California diver occassionally can have the thrill of approaching and scratching the fish, which sometimes seems to enjoy the rubdown. Fishermen have seen gulls and other sea birds perched on top of floating Mola Molas, pecking off parasites.

photo by Bob Evans

Photo was taken in 35 feet of water off Southern California coast. Evans used a Nikon F camera with a 24mm lens, Subsea strobe, and High Speed Ektachrome film. Shot at 1/60 second at f/18, 4 feet from subject.

Bibliography

Axelrod, H.R., and C.W. Emmens. *Exotic Marine Fishes*. Neptune City, NJ: T.F.H. Publications, 1968.

Baxter, J.L. *Inshore Fishes of California*. Sacramento: California Department of Fish and Game, 1966.

Beebe, W., and J. Tee-Van. *Field Book of the Shore Fishes of Bermuda and the West Indies*. Mineola, NY: Dover Press, 1970.

Böhlke, J.E., and C.C.G. Chaplin. *Fishes of the Bahamas and Adjacent Tropical Waters*. Wynnewood, PA: Livingston Publishing Co., 1968.

Bridges, W. *New York Aquarium Book of the Water World*. New York: American Heritage Press, 1970.

Burgess, W., and H. Axelrod. *Pacific Marine Fishes*. Neptune, NJ: T.F.H. Publications, 1974. 5 vols.

Chaplin, C.C.G., and P. Scott. *Fishwatcher's Guide to West Atlantic Coral Reefs*. Wynnewood, PA: Livingston Publishing Co., 1972.

Chute, W.H. *Shedd Aquarium Guide*. Chicago: Shedd Aquarium Society, 1960.

Clemens, W.A., and G.V. Wilby. *Fishes of the Pacific Coast and Canada*. Ottawa: Fisheries Research Board of Canada, 1949.

Coleman, N. *Australian Sea Fishes*. Sidney: Doubleday Australia Pty. Ltd., 1980.

Eschmeyer, William N., and E.S. Herald. *A Field Guide to Pacific Coast Fishes of North America*. Boston: Houghton Mifflin Co., 1983.

Fitch, J.E., and R.J. Lavenberg. *Tidepool and Nearshore Fishes of California*. Berkeley: University of California Press, 1975.

———. *Marine Food and Game Fishes of California*. Berkeley: University of California Press, 1971.

Frank, S., and A. Wheeler. *The Pictorial Encyclopaedia of Fishes*. London: Hamlyn Publishing Group, Ltd., 1971.

Gosline, W.A., and V.E. Brock. *Handbook of Hawaiian Fishes*. Honolulu: University of Hawaii Press, 1960.

Gotshall, D.W. *Fishwatcher's Guide to the Inshore Fishes of the Pacific Coast*. Los Osos, CA: Sea Challengers, 1977.

Grant, E.M. *Guide to Fishes*. Brisbane, Australia: Department of Harbours and Marine, Brisbane, Queensland, 1978.

Hart, J.L. *Pacific Fishes of Canada*. Ottawa: Fisheries Research Board of Canada, 1973.

Hobson, E., and E.H. Chave. *Hawaiian Reef Animals*. Honolulu: University of Hawaii Press, 1972.

Jaeger, E.C. *A Source-book of Biological Names and Terms*. Springfield, IL: Charles C. Thomas, 1978.

Marshall, T. *Tropical Fishes of the Great Barrier Reef*. New York: American Elsevier Publishing Co., 1966.

Masuda, H., C. Araga, and T. Yoshino. *Coastal Fishes of Southern Japan*. Tokyo: Tokai University Press, 1975.

Miller, D.J., and R.N. Lea. *Guide to the Coastal Marine Fishes of California*. State of California Department of Fish and Game, Bulletin No. 157. Sacramento: 1972.

North, W.J. *Underwater California*. Berkeley: University of California Press, 1976.

Phillips, J.B. *A Review of the Rockfishes of California (family Scorpaenidae)*. Sacramento: State of California Department of Fish and Game, 1972.

Randall, J.E. *Caribbean Reef Fishes*. Neptune City, NJ: T.F.H. Publications, 1968.

———. *Food Habits of Reef Fishes of the West Indies*. Coral Gables: University of Miami Institute of Marine Science Publications, 1967.

———. *Red Sea Reef Fishes*. London: Scorpion Communications and Publications, Ltd., 1983.

———. *Underwater Guide to Hawaiian Reef Fishes*. Valley Forge, PA: Harrowood Books, 1981.

Ray, C., and E. Ciampi. *The Underwater Guide to Marine Life*. San Diego, CA: A.S. Barnes, 1956.

Roedel, P.M. *Common Ocean Fishes of the California Coast*. State of California Department of Fish and Game, Bulletin No. 91. Sacramento: 1953.

Stokes, F.J. *Handguide to the Coral Reef Fishes of the Caribbean*. Philadelphia: Lippincott and Crowell, 1980.

Thomson, D.A., L.T. Findley, and A.N. Kerstich. *Reef Fishes of the Sea of Cortez*. New York: John Wiley and Sons, 1979.

Tinker, S. *Hawaiian Fishes*. Honolulu: Tongg Publishing Co., 1944.

Zeiller, W. *Tropical Marine Fishes*. San Diego, CA: A.S. Barnes, 1975.

Index